KENT MURDER AND MAYHEM

Kent
Murder
& Mayhem

Roy Ingleton

Wharncliffe Books

First published in Great Britain in 2008 by
Wharncliffe Local History
an imprint of
Pen and Sword Books Limited,
47 Church Street, Barnsley,
South Yorkshire. S70 2AS

Copyright © Roy Ingleton, 2008

ISBN: 978 1 84563 059 1

Typeset in Plantin and Benguiat by
Pen and Sword Books Ltd

Printed in the United Kingdom by
CPI UK

Pen & Sword Books Ltd incorporates the imprints of
Pen & Sword Aviation, Pen & Sword Maritime,
Pen & Sword Military, Wharncliffe Local History, Pen & Sword Select,
Pen & Sword Military Classics and Leo Cooper.

For a complete list of Pen & Sword titles please contact:
PEN & SWORD BOOKS LIMITED
47 Church Street, Barnsley, South Yorkshire, S70 2AS, England.
E-mail: enquiries@pen-and-sword.co.uk
Website: www.pen-and-sword.co.uk

Contents

Introduction and Acknowledgements

Kent has been known as the 'Garden of England' since time immemorial, a soubriquet bestowed on the county in recognition of the bountiful apple and cherry orchards, the quintessential hop gardens, the lush pastures of the Romney marsh and other agricultural and horticultural delights. Hardly the place, one might think, for dark deeds and grisly retribution, but the reader will see that the county has indeed had its more sombre side over the centuries.

Over the years, numerous sturdy Kentish countrymen (and women) met their end by poisoning, battering, drowning, shooting, stabbing and every other conceivable *modus operandi*. In return, Penenden Heath, the ancient Anglo-Saxon meeting place and site of one of the country's earliest courts, was for centuries also the place where countless criminals met their end on the gallows. Indeed, many of the murderers referred to in this book felt the noose around their neck as they gazed for the last time upon the peaceful Kentish countryside surrounding the Heath. Others suffered the same fate at the less bucolic atmosphere of Maidstone Prison, whether outside in public or inside in relative privacy.

This book, then, recounts some of their stories, and my thanks are extended to the staff of the Centre for Kentish Studies and of the various branches of the Kent Arts and Libraries Department for their unstinting support and assistance. Most of the photographs are the author's own and, so far as the others are concerned, acknowledgement has been given or permission sought wherever it has been possible to trace the copyright holders. My apologies are given in advance to those concerned if there has been any oversight, with an assurance that this will be corrected in future editions.

Chapter 1

'The Place of Execution . . .'

The sleepy residential area on the outskirts of Maidstone known as Penenden Heath is the picture of suburban calm and tranquillity. Pleasant villas and a traditional English pub surround a large green on which the locals exercise their dogs and play cricket in the summer. It is the sort of village suburb celebrated in the poetry of Sir John Betjeman, and the kind of place John Major spoke about: 'Fifty years from now, Britain will still be the country of long shadows on cricket grounds, warm beer, invincible green suburbs, dog lovers and pools fillers.'

But it was not always so. For more centuries than one can imagine, this large expanse of open heathland, nestling under the North Downs, was the traditional county meeting place. In Anglo-Saxon times it was the location of the shire court, where justice was dispensed in matters of some significance, a practice which continued after the arrival of the Normans.

In 1076, Archbishop Lanfranc brought a successful lawsuit against Odo, Bishop of Bayeux and Earl of Kent, regarding some land within the diocese of Canterbury which he alleged Odo had purloined. Such was the importance attached to tradition that Æthelric, the elderly former bishop of Selsey, was brought to Penenden Heath in a cart to advise on Anglo-Saxon law.

When Wat Tyler led a march on London in 1381 to protest about the treatment of the English peasants, he gathered his protesters and began his march on Penenden Heath.

Still later, during the English Civil War, the main Royalist forces in the county under the Earl of Norwich were assembled on Penenden Heath when the Parliamentarian army under the Lord General Fairfax advanced on Maidstone.

But, for the purposes of this book, Penenden Heath's claim to fame is a much darker one. With the shire court being held there

Penenden Heath as it appeared in Hasted's Map of 1797. The County Court can be seen to the north of the Heath and the site of the gallows was to the south. Kent County Library, Springfield.

and, later, the assize court sitting in the nearby county town of Maidstone, the unfortunate felons convicted at these courts of justice knew that Penenden Heath was to be their place of execution.

During the seventeenth, eighteenth and nineteenth centuries in particular, an astonishing number of men, women and even young boys were hanged on the gallows on the Heath, many for such trifling crimes as the theft of a silk kerchief or some other item valued at twelve pence (5p) or more.

Even by the comparatively enlightened times of the beginning of the nineteenth century, the number of persons condemned to death was staggering by modern standards. At one sitting of the Kent Assizes in 1801, no fewer than thirty-seven felons were sentenced to death. It is true that half of these were reprieved and their sentence commuted to one of transportation to Australia for life, but the rest were transported the couple of miles to the Heath where they were hanged by the neck until they were dead.

Until the middle of the nineteenth century it was the tradition that hangings were always carried out in public, whether on Tyburn Hill or indeed in Kent. The authorities were convinced that the sight of some poor wretch kicking and struggling on the end of a rope would be a salutary lesson to any would-be miscreants gathered at the place of execution. In fact, the public on the whole regarded a hanging as an enjoyable form of free public entertainment. Large crowds would foregather to hear the victim's last words and to make a considered judgement on how they met their end. Were the felons penitent? Did they ask for God's forgiveness? Was their bearing correct and stoical or did they become hysterical and fight against the hangman? A good hanging could be the main subject of conversation for days afterwards in the coffee houses and drinking dens in the town and surrounding villages.

Public executions had taken place on Penenden Heath for probably more than a millennium but, in 1830, the new Maidstone Prison was opened and henceforth executions would take place outside the prison. This saved the authorities the chore (not to mention the security risk) of carting the condemned person to the

Maidstone Prison, from an old engraving, c.1840.

Heath, but the executions were still performed in public. In fact, the removal of the place of execution to the centre of the town made the 'entertainment' much more accessible; now even the halt and the lame could struggle on their crutches or in their Bath chairs to witness the enthralling events.

A total of fifty-eight condemned prisoners were executed at Maidstone Prison, twenty-eight of whom were hanged in public outside the prison walls. The scaffold was erected beside the main gate of the prison the day before the event and consisted of a raised platform, in the centre of which were the trapdoors. In the middle stood a simple structure of two stout uprights supporting a cross-beam, on which there was a hook to which the noose would be attached. The prisoner and escort would mount the platform by means of a short flight of steps, and the lower part of the scaffold was draped in black cloth to hide the legs of the usually struggling prisoner. Following countless botched executions, a new type of gallows was introduced in the 1880s, based on a design by Lieutenant Colonel Alten Beamish, RE, of the Home Office Surveyors' Department, whereby the trap was opened by a lever-operated drawbar which proved infallible.

By 1841 thieves, arsonists and similar, less serious, felons were being sent to prison, rather than subjected to the ultimate penalty. By convention, only convicted murderers and traitors were now being hanged, a situation which was ratified by law in 1861. Although the number of executions was accordingly reduced, there were still enough murderers to provide entertainment for the crowds. Not until 1868 was the public spectacle abolished by the Capital Punishment Amendment Act, after which executions were carried out inside the prison, away from the eyes of the public.

The execution of the sentence of death was devolved on the county sheriffs and, in the early days, the hangman was usually some local worthy who was willing to undertake the task, often with disastrous results. Not until 1829 was a public executioner appointed with nationwide responsibilities, although a number of executions continued to be carried out by ad hoc hangmen employed by the sheriffs.

The condemned cell.

The first public hangman was one William Calcraft, who was paid a yearly retainer of £20 by the Sheriffs of London and was used by several other authorities, including Kent. Calcraft would therefore travel down from London to Maidstone to carry out his grisly task as and when his services were required. Since this was before the railways arrived, the journey would have to be made by stagecoach and the discomfort would have done little to improve the hangman's temper.

In early times, the condemned man stood on a stool or box which was kicked away to leave him dangling on the end of the rope but, by the time of Calcraft's appointment, the 'drop' type of gallows, in which a trapdoor under the victim's feet was opened to send him to eternity, was in general use. However, the drop was short, which usually meant that the condemned man or woman slowly strangled to death. In an interview the long-retired Calcraft gave to the *Cassells Saturday Journal* (23 January 1892), he was asked if he was ever upset by his task:

> *'No, not a bit. Why should I be? I am only doing my duty,' replied the hangman.*
>
> *'Still, it is a very dreadful duty; and even as a matter of duty, few persons could kill a man without …'*
>
> *'Kill a man!' broke in the elderly executioner. 'Who kills a man? I never killed a man.'*
>
> *There was a momentary embarrassment for his questioner, and then Calcraft proceeded to explain, 'They kills themselves. I merely put a rope round their necks and knock away the platform beneath them.'*
>
> *He then remarked emphatically, 'I don't kill 'em; it's their own weight as does it.'*

Despite these comments, it is clear that, on a number of occasions, Calcraft had to descend below the trapdoor and hang on the legs of the struggling, strangling victim to hasten his demise. His reputation as a hangman was not a particularly good one.

Calcraft presided over a number of executions on Penenden Heath and at the Maidstone Prison during the forty-five years he was the official executioner, and he was responsible for the execution of many of the murderers whose deeds are described in

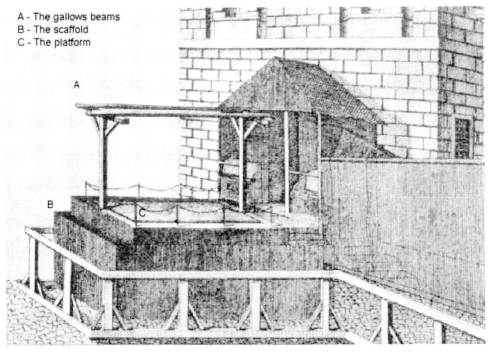

A - The gallows beams
B - The scaffold
C - The platform

A

B

C

The prison gallows.

this book. His last assignment on Penenden Heath was on Christmas Eve 1830, when he hanged three farm workers for arson, a felony committed as part of the 'Swing' riots against the conditions facing agricultural workers.

Calcraft was not a man of science or invention and it was left to his successor, William Marwood (1872–83) to devise the 'long drop', by means of which most hanged persons died from a broken neck. The only danger with this innovation was that, if the drop was not carefully calculated, the victim could end up being decapitated. Over the years the mechanics of hanging developed until, by the time the last death sentence was carried out in August 1964, it was a swift and comparatively merciful end, the drop resulting in almost instantaneous death.

Chapter 2

Boiled Alive

No form of execution is painless but some forms are more barbaric than others. Fortunately, Britain has been spared the worst excesses of Caligula, Vlad the Impaler, Torquemada, Idi Amin and other notorious tyrants but, even so, our history includes some pretty dreadful means of punishing the wrongdoer.

High treason, for example, was traditionally punished by the prolonged and agonizing practice of hanging, drawing and quartering which consisted of the condemned man being drawn on a hurdle to the place of execution, hanged by the neck until almost dead, disembowelled and his genitalia and entrails burned before his eyes, before finally being beheaded and the corpse divided into four quarters. This form of execution was confined to the male sex; women were 'merely' burned at the stake.

Originally reserved for enemies of the state, the first recorded case was that of the Welsh prince, Dafydd ap Gruffydd (1243), during the reign of Edward I, followed not too long afterwards by the Scottish leader, William 'Braveheart' Wallace. The charge of high treason and its dreadful punishment were extended over the years to papists and counterfeiters or coiners, as well as those who took liberties with the king's wife, such as Francis Dereham, the lover of Catherine Howard.

However, because of circumstances which arose in the twenty-second year of his reign, King Henry VIII extended the scope of this ultimate crime to include cases of murder by poisoning. He further expressly decreed that the penalty for this form of treason should be boiling alive, a gruesome form of execution widely used in Europe between the thirteenth and sixteenth centuries, especially in France and Germany, but virtually unknown in England.

Boiled alive. From a very old engraving.

The Gunpowder Plotters being hanged, drawn and quartered. From a contemporary engraving.

Although poisoning is often seen as a woman's means of getting rid of her husband or other unwanted friends and relatives, the first and deliberately intended victim of this Special Act was a Kent man. Uniquely, the Act named him as the first person against whom the punishment was to be applied.

The unfortunate man was one Richard Rouse, who had been employed as a cook in the Lambeth palace of John Fisher, the Bishop of Rochester. One of the meals he prepared for the Bishop and his family apparently contained some noxious substance which caused the death of one of the diners and severely incapacitated numerous others. It was the Bishop's practice to have the leftovers from his table given to the poor of the parish and, on this occasion, some of these were stricken down as well. The possibility of one of the governing class being poisoned in his own home was too frightful to contemplate and the King had to ensure that, insofar as was possible, nothing like this could happen in the future – and the best protection was a horrendously severe form of execution.

And so a Special Act of Parliament was passed in 1531 which, after the usual lengthy preamble, emphasized that murder was 'most highly to be detested and abhorred; and especially all kinds of murder by poisoning', even though this type of murder was very rare.

The Act went on to describe how:

> *one Richard Rouse, late of Rochester in the County of Kent, cook, otherwise called Richard Cook, … did cast a certain venom or poison into a vessel replenished with yeast or balm, standing in the kitchen of the reverend father in God, John, Bishop of Rochester, at his palace in Lambeth Marsh; with which yeast or balm … porridge or gruel was forthwith made for the family there being; whereby not only the number of seventeen persons of his said family, which did eat of that porridge, were mortally infected or poisoned, and one of them, that is to say Bennet Curwan, gentleman, is thereof deceased; but also certain poor people which resorted to the said bishop's palace and were there charitably fed with remains of the said porridge … were likewise infected and one poor woman of them, … is also thereof now deceased.*
>
> *Our Sovereign lord the King … abhorring all such abominable offences, because in that manner no person can live in surety out of danger of death by that means, hath ordained and enacted … that the said poisoning be adjudged and deemed as high treason; and that the said Richard, for the said murder and poisoning of the said two persons shall stand and be attainted of high treason.*
>
> *And … it is ordained … that the said Richard Rouse shall therefore be boiled to death … and that from henceforth every wilful murder … committed or done by means or way of poisoning, shall be reputed, deemed and judged in law to be high treason; and that all … indicted and condemned … of such treason shall be immediately after such attainder or condemnation, committed to execution of death by boiling for the same.*

And so, a few days later, poor Richard Rouse of Rochester was bound and placed in a cauldron over a fire and boiled to death at Smithfield. This method of execution being a great novelty, a large crowd made its way to the place of execution and the spectators were no doubt duly impressed by what they saw.

Shortly afterwards, two women suffered this same fate; one was boiled to death in King's Lynn, Norfolk, also in 1531, for poisoning her husband while another, Margaret Davey, was similarly boiled alive, also in Smithfield, in 1542. These may well have been the last to suffer this fate.

One can easily understand why the ruling classes were terrified of murder or assassination by such means. Their meals were prepared by their poorly paid and often ill-treated social inferiors, many of whom might harbour a grudge or be open to a bribe from a political or religious enemy. The poison could so easily be administered by mixing it with food or drink, the strong flavour of which in Tudor times was likely to conceal the taste of the poison. Bodyguards might protect the target from knife or sword but they were powerless against this insidious and invisible death threat.

Was Richard Rouse guilty of the crime for which he was so cruelly put to death? He does not appear to have confessed and, in any case, confessions obtained by means of torture – as they usually were in those days – are scarcely reliable evidence. What was the poison used? How did Rouse obtain it? What was his motive? None of these questions seem to have been answered, assuming they were ever asked.

Given the understanding of toxicology half a millennium ago, how could the doctors be so sure that poison was in fact used? With our more modern level of knowledge we might wonder whether the actual cause of death and malaise was simply straightforward food-poisoning – botulism, salmonella, listeria, clostridium, or the like. One can imagine the level of hygiene in a Tudor kitchen. Perhaps all poor Richard Rouse was guilty of was failing to wash his hands.

An alternative explanation could be that, as John Fisher, in common with many other clerics at the time, was opposed to Henry's divorce and to the King's plans to be recognized as the head of the Church in England, he was becoming a nuisance – and Henry's solution for troublesome priests was simply to get rid of them. It is therefore entirely possible that there was indeed an assassination attempt, but one which was instigated by the King himself and poor Richard was simply a scapegoat.

What is certain, however, is that the reverend Bishop of Rochester was beheaded four years later in the Tower of London, shortly before the Archbishop of Canterbury met the same fate.

Chapter 3

The Gentlemen Go By

If you wake at midnight, and hear a horse's feet,
Don't go drawing back the blind, or looking in the street.
Them that asks no questions isn't told a lie,
Watch the wall, my darling, while the Gentlemen go by!
Five and twenty ponies, trotting through the dark,
Brandy for the parson, 'baccy for the clerk;
Laces for a lady, letters for a spy,
And watch the wall my darling, while the Gentlemen go by!

Rudyard Kipling, 'A Smuggler's Song'

An unwise traveller, walking or riding in the vicinity of Kingsgate on the Isle of Thanet in the early hours of a cold, foggy morning in March 1769 might, if he were very unfortunate, have stumbled upon a band of men standing or crouching on the cliff top, looking out over the so-called Botany Bay. Unfortunate, because this was the ruthless Callis Court Gang of smugglers, feared throughout Thanet and beyond and any stranger would automatically be assumed to be on the side of the revenue men and his life forfeit.

A signal light shone from the sea, answered by the light of another lantern, carefully and cunningly masked, shining seawards from the shore. The coast was clear and the armed lugger *Lark* drew closer to the shore, where it dropped anchor. A small boat drew away, heavily laden with all manner of contraband: lace, tea, gin, brandy, tobacco and many other heavily taxed items. The crew of six drew the boat up onto the shingle and were met by the shore-based smugglers, leading a team of packhorses.

The transfer of the goods from boat to horseback was quickly and efficiently accomplished, evidence of considerable experience, and the last packages were being secured when a loud voice cried out, 'Halt! In the name of the King I command you to halt!' The Excise patrol, tipped off by an informer, had been lying in wait.

But the smugglers were not going to surrender easily and a fierce fight broke out between the two parties. The still night air was shattered by the clash of cutlasses, the reports of muskets and pistols and the cries of the wounded, some of whom had been mortally injured.

The leader of the gang, Joss Snelling, together with four of his men, made good their escape through an opening in the cliff and made their way to the top, only to be confronted by a lone officer. Without hesitation, the unfortunate man was gunned down and the escaping smugglers made their way to Reading Street, about half a mile away.

The battle over, the Excise men escorted eight prisoners to the *Captain Digby Inn*, an isolated and lonely hostelry on the edge of the cliff, carrying their mortally wounded comrade with them. He was the only fatality among the King's men, although several had been wounded. As for the smugglers, apart from the eight prisoners, ten of their comrades were lying dead in the surf. Perhaps they were the lucky ones, since the prisoners were tried, convicted and sentenced to death and ultimately hanged on Gallows Field, Sandwich.

There was no evidence to convict the gang's leader, 28-year-old Snelling, although several of the Excise men thought they had recognized him at the scene. Snelling had lost most of his gang but, within a year, he had formed another nearly twice the size. He continued to operate in the area for a number of years, earning the nickname 'the Broadstairs Smuggler'. Whether nearby Joss Bay is named after him, or whether he took his pseudonym from his favourite landing place has been hotly disputed over the years. In 1829 the elderly Joss Snelling was presented to the future Queen Victoria as 'the famous Broadstairs smuggler' and went on to live to the ripe old age of 96, a good age by any standard but an exceptional one for someone who was for so long involved in the dangerous and ruthless pastime of smuggling.

Joss Snelling's story is but one of many associated with smuggling in Kent. With around three-quarters of the county surrounded by sea and given its closeness to the continent of Europe, it is not surprising that Kent was (and perhaps still is) a favoured place for smuggling. The heyday for this activity was in the eighteenth and early nineteenth centuries, when smuggling was a regular sideline for local sailors and fishermen. Soon large gangs were almost permanently engaged in bringing contraband goods into England

and making a very handsome living by it.

Although often romanticized in literature and folklore, this illegal traffic could, as we have seen, often become violent and vicious and the government made strenuous efforts to suppress it. Such were the numbers involved on both sides that the conflicts between them could, at times, be accurately described as a battle. Apart from the Battle of Botany Bay, notable incidents included the 'battles' of Lydd (1721), Stonecrouch (1733), Sandwich Bay (1746), Goudhurst (1747), Whitstable (1780), Sandgate (1820), Hampton and Brookland (both 1821).

Between 1817 and 1831, the Royal Navy provided a blockade force of 1,480 armed men, stationed at various points between Sheerness and West Sussex and this appears to have had a significant effect, certainly on large-scale illicit importations and the pitched battles of the past.

Apart from Joss Snelling, there were a number of notable characters engaged in this illegal trade in Kent, such as Richard Joy, the 'Kentish Giant', reputed to stand over seven feet tall and weighing in at well over twenty stone. A farm labourer from Whitstable, he was caught smuggling and avoided the death penalty by being pressed into the Navy, where he was renowned for carrying a loaded cannon across the ship's deck for a wager. It took six men to replace it. Joy eventually returned to his old tricks and was drowned on another smuggling run at the age of 67 and is buried in St Peter's churchyard in Broadstairs.

Another character was Samuel Jackson – 'Slippery Sam' – who, born in 1730, very soon embarked on a life of crime, including involvement in smuggling, like his father before him. He was obviously quite successful as, at the age of 20, he purchased the freehold of a farmhouse on the Stone Street at Petham, between Canterbury and Hythe. This house, under which he stored and hid his illicit goods in a maze of tunnels, still exists; it is known, not surprisingly as Slippery Sam's and has been used in recent years as a restaurant.

Sam's nickname came about as a result of a daring escape he made from the old Maidstone Gaol by stripping and covering his body in axle grease, enabling him to slip through a small window opening. His career was short-lived, however, as in 1760 he was hanged for shooting and killing a revenue officer and his body was hung in a gibbet as a warning to others.

In 1745 Deal was already infamous as a centre for smuggling. One contemporary writer, Fanny Burney, penned,

There are said to be in the town of Deal, not less than two hundred young men and sea-faring people, who are known to have no visible way of getting a living, but by the infamous trade of smuggling …
This smuggling has converted those employed in it, first from honest, industrious fishermen, to lazy, drunken and profligate smugglers.

Such was the notoriety of the town that, in 1781 a military operation involving nine hundred infantrymen and a hundred cavalry descended on the town, but this had only limited success as the townsfolk were expecting them and had spirited the contraband goods away. Three years later, a further military expedition burned all the town's fishing boats as retribution for their owners' illicit activities.

Much as tax evasion today is not regarded by many to be a real crime, since the only loser is seen to be the government, so smuggling was widely accepted and exploited by the people in Kentish coastal towns and villages, not to mention many of the professional classes and nobility at that time. The Member of Parliament for the City of Canterbury, Sir Thomas Hardress, KC, was known as the 'Smugglers' Friend' because of the large number of smugglers he successfully defended in the last quarter of the eighteenth century. There have also been suggestions that Sir Edward Knatchbull (1781–1849), magistrate and pillar of Kent society, may have had associations with the smugglers, as many of his decisions seemed to favour them, enabling them to escape the death penalty. His intervention prevented the body of Cephas Quested being hung in chains at Brookland and ensured that it was instead quietly buried in Aldington. His apparent leniency towards so-called 'Swing Rioters' also aroused adverse comments from many, including Sir Robert Peel, the Home Secretary.

Perhaps the most famous of the early smuggling bands was the so-called Hawkhurst Gang, which had its base at the *Oak and Ivy* public house in that town, only a few miles from the Romney Marshes. The concept of a 'gang' was a rather vague one as there

The Oak and Ivy *public house, Hawkhurst.* Photo © copyright Kent Messenger Group.

was probably only a handful of more-or-less permanent smugglers, the remainder being made up from a wide circle of willing helpers. It has been reported that the Hawkhurst Gang could call upon the services of some five hundred men for a particular operation. Two separate incidents marked the end of this gang: the power and influence of the gang in the nearby village of Goudhurst provoked a great deal of resentment, and a former soldier, George Sturt, formed a militia group to defend the village and keep the smugglers out. A fierce battle ensued in which the smugglers were repulsed, leaving three of their number dead. The second event was the callous and brutal murder of a customs officer and a prosecution witness he was escorting. The general public was so horrified by this killing and by the viciousness and general lawlessness of the gang that information was leaked to the authorities and the leaders of the gang were arrested and executed in 1747, their bodies being hung in chains at various places in the county where they were well known.

However, although their activities were either ignored (by people 'turning their faces to the wall') or actively encouraged, the major smuggling gangs were quite ruthless and would not hesitate to kill any revenue officer or trooper who stood in their way. With groups of around 250 smugglers and their helpers unloading the contraband, the revenue officers, even with the support of a squadron of dragoons, were at a great disadvantage against such a determined mob. It was not until after the end of the Napoleonic wars in 1816 that the government had enough money, ships and manpower to really wage war on this activity and set up a blockade around the Kent and Sussex coasts, supported by galleys and cutters which patrolled the English Channel. With such a force opposing them, the smugglers had themselves to become more organized, more ruthless if they were to succeed. The golden days of the part-time, amateur smuggler were over and large, semi-professional bands began to be formed.

One highly successful and dangerous gang which emerged was known as the Aldington Gang, which was based in the *Walnut Tree Inn* in the village of Aldington, on the edge of the Romney Marsh and working the coast between Rye and Dover in the 1820s. Its leader was a strong and intelligent man by the name of George Ransley, who came from a family of criminals. His two cousins, James and William, were also smugglers but ended up on the gallows at Penenden Heath, charged with highway robbery. The grave board for the Ransley family can still be seen in the churchyard in Ruckinge.

Much of George Ransley's success may be put down to his highly developed organizational skills and an almost military discipline which he demanded of his followers. While one section of the gang speedily unloaded the cargo, another section stood guard with muskets and cutlasses. Once the contraband was stowed on the carts or packhorses, the escort would follow the procession to protect its rear. A policy of never leaving a wounded smuggler to be captured and interrogated ensured both the loyalty of the men and the secrecy of the casualties involved. The proceeds from the smuggling would pay for a doctor (who knew better than to ask too many questions) and provide some financial support for the family of the wounded member of the gang.

Of course, the smugglers were never described as such: George Ransley was ostensibly a farmer who also ran an illicit drinking house, where some of the smuggled liquor could be sampled. His house, which is still standing and occupied, was known as the Bourne Tap and brought him in a very handsome income.

The Aldington Gang first came to the notice of the authorities in November 1820 when a galley laden to the gunwales with contraband spirits and tobacco came ashore at Sandgate. A crowd of some 250 men was awaiting its arrival, already formed into three groups, one to unload the cargo and two to act as their protectors. Not surprisingly, such a large gathering did not escape the notice of members of the blockade force, two of whom challenged the smugglers and were promptly attacked and badly wounded for their pains. The noise attracted two other naval men, one of whom was quickly captured by the mob while the other bravely fired into the crowd and brandished his cutlass, despite being wounded in the leg. Such efforts, while supremely courageous, did little to deter the crowd, which swiftly made off with the cargo. The captured man was released the next day.

A couple of months later, another illicit landing was made at Camber Sands, between Rye in Sussex and Lydd in Kent. Once more over two hundred men were involved but this time they were intercepted by a strong government force which chased them across the marshes to Brookland. A fierce battle ensued, later to be described in local folklore as the 'Battle of Brookland', in which five men (four smugglers and one blockade man) died and more than twenty were wounded. Two of the smugglers were detained, one of whom declared he was merely an innocent bystander and was acquitted. The other prisoner was one Cephas Quested, who was alleged to have been one of the ringleaders. During the mêlée on the beach, Quested handed a musket to a young man standing beside him, assuming he was one of the gang and told him to 'blow an officer's brains out'. But the man was in fact a Royal Navy midshipman who gratefully took the weapon and promptly turned it on Quested and arrested him. Despite a rigorous interrogation, he refused to 'grass' on his colleagues and turn King's Evidence and so was convicted and hanged at Penenden Heath on 4 July 1821.

The Aldington Gang frequently used to store their cargoes in the ancient Augustinian priory at Bilsington, which was then used as a farmhouse, and a number of ghost stories were circulated in order to deter inquisitive locals. Although often brutal and vicious, the gang evidently had a rather black sense of humour, as was demonstrated when a captured officer was blindfolded and cast off a cliff top. With his legs dangling over the edge, the poor man managed to cling on to a few tufts of grass to save himself from falling to what he believed would be certain death but eventually his fingers tired and he released his hold – to fall all of six inches onto the beach below.

Dover was another favoured landing place for smuggled goods and in 1820 a revenue officer known as Billy 'Hellfire' Lilburn, on the Excise cutter *Lively*, caught a galley with eleven Folkestone and Sandgate smugglers off Dover. The facts were fully described in the *Kentish Gazette* on 30 May 1820:

> *ten of them being found fit for the navy, the whole were committed to Dover gaol until the ten could be removed to some of His Majesty's receiving ships. ... from the vast influx of ill-looking men* [it was thought] *that a rescue would be attempted and every precaution was taken ... to guard against it by having a body of constables, the seamen belonging to the preventive service and a detachment of military, drawn up both inside and out-side the gaol.*
>
> *The time of removal was 12 o'clock, but two hours before that a large body had collected together which continued increasing every minute and ... several hundreds were collected in front and at every avenue leading to the gaol, with every disposition to riot and rescue.*

The Mayor and another magistrate attended the scene and gave the constables strict instructions to keep the peace and to the seamen and soldiers not to charge 'unless absolutely driven to do so'. The newspaper report continues:

> *The door of the prison was opened and the smugglers just on the point of being brought out when a general shout was sent up by the crowd of 'Liberty for ever!' and a number of stones and brickbats were thrown at them.*

Drawing of Dover beach in the eighteenth century.

Things became so serious that the Mayor directed that the removal of the prisoners be suspended for the time being, which was a prudent move.

> *The mob being foiled in their attempt to rescue the prisoners proceeded to further acts of violence and, notwithstanding that the Riot Act was twice read from the gaol window by the Mayor, commenced an attack on the gaol with crowbars, pick-axes, hammers, saws, etc., unroofed the top and threw part of the side wall down and not only released the whole of the 11 smugglers but several*

other prisoners confined in the gaol under sentence; and they succeeded in getting them clear off, the imposing number of the mob intimidated the peace officers and others from acting. One of the persons most active in the riot was taken and placed in a chaise with two constables, to be conveyed to St Augustine's Gaol at Canterbury; but a mob collected at the end of the town, stopped the chaise, dragged the rioter and constables out and notwithstanding the former was hand-cuffed to the latter, the mob threw the constables to the ground, and severing the hand-cuff with a cold chisel, released the rioter. After the release of the smugglers, who all belong to Folkestone, the crowd dispersed and the town remained tranquil.

A few days later, the following notice appeared in the *Kentish Gazette*:

Friday, June 2nd 1820
DOVER
WHEREAS on FRIDAY last, the 26th May, a very numerous lawless and desperate GANG of SMUGGLERS, disguised in round Frocks, as Countrymen, and armed with Bludgeons, and many of them with concealed Fire-arms, assembled round His Majesty's Gaol at Dover, and having provided themselves with pick-axes, crow bars, and other implements, proceeded in a most daring and tumultuous manner, feloniously to BREAK and ENTER the back part of the GAOL, and released therefrom, [there followed a list of names], *eleven Smugglers, all Natives or Inhabitants of Folkestone, who were confined in the said Gaol*

—

Whoever will give information to Sir Thomas MANTELL, Mayor of Dover, so that any one or more of the person or persons guilty of the said daring outrage and felony may be brought to justice, shall receive a reward of
ONE HUNDRED POUNDS
And whoever will apprehend and bring to His Majesty's Gaol at Dover, any of the eleven Smugglers thus lawlessly released, shall receive a reward of FIFTY POUNDS for every Smuggler so apprehended and brought to Gaol
By order of the Mayor and Justices.

The Bourne Tap, Aldington.

The gaol, which was situated on the south side of the Market Place near the Guildhall, was so badly damaged a new one had to be built.

A similar, albeit smaller-scale riot occurred in Folkestone, also in 1820, when a blockade man by the name of John Kelty arrested a smuggler in possession of a tub of spirits and took him to the nearby watch house (probably the one at the bottom of the Bayle Steps). Before he could arrange for the prisoner to be removed to more secure accommodation, an armed mob broke in, injured Kelty and released the prisoner.

The success of the Aldington Gang, like any other, depended on the support and goodwill of the local populace, but some members grew to believe themselves beyond any law and engaged in housebreaking and burglary and other crimes against the local inhabitants, and their support dwindled away. With a large price on the heads of the ringleaders, it was only a matter of time before someone would wreak their revenge and inform the authorities. And so, when a popular local naval quartermaster was killed by the gang, and another wounded on the beach at Dover, the large reward offered was claimed by several informants.

The information received proved invaluable and one night in October 1826, a substantial group of blockade men, accompanied by two Bow Street Runners, surrounded George Ransley's house at the Bourne Tap. The guard dogs were quickly disposed of and Ransley was arrested, still in his nightshirt, and a further seven smugglers were apprehended.

Also as a result of the information received, within a few weeks a total of nineteen had been arrested and were tried at the Maidstone Assizes for a number of serious, capital crimes. Found guilty, all were sentenced to death but, thanks to the intervention of their astute lawyer, they were reprieved and transported to Australia

Graveboard of the notorious Ransley family in Ruckinge churchyard.

instead. George Ransley's knowledge of farming stood him in good stead and in due course he was granted a ticket of leave and permitted to send for his wife and family. It is understood that he went on to live to a ripe old age in Van Diemen's Land (Tasmania).

This prosecution signalled the end of the Aldington Gang, the reputation of which was later enhanced by the publication of the *Adventures of Dr Syn* by Russell Thorndyke. It was also effectively the end of large-scale smuggling in Kent.

Chapter 4

Burned at the Stake

The ancient borough of Hythe, one of the original Cinque Ports, lying sleepily near to Folkestone on the Kent coast, does not give the impression of having witnessed anything more serious than a runaway horse and cart, or the odd drunken brawl, but this impression is entirely erroneous.

Even the parish church of St Leonard is famous for a macabre reason: the crypt houses the mortal remains of some 4,000 men, women and children, the 2,000 skulls and 8,000 femurs neatly stacked on shelves, open to public display.

The town itself has suffered fire and flood, smuggling and sudden death. It was also the scene of the last execution of a woman in England by burning at the stake, which is where our story begins.

John Lott was a wealthy grazier and butcher, living on the outskirts of the town. A single man, he needed someone to keep house and prepare his meals and so, in 1766, he took on an attractive young girl by the name of Susannah as a general maidservant. Over the next two years John Lott became more and more enamoured with this young woman and went so far as to propose to her on several occasions, being rejected each time. So persistent was he in his pursuit of the maidservant that she eventually decided her position was becoming untenable and so she left his employ and went to live with her sister in Rolvenden.

During Susannah's stay in Rolvenden she met the brother of her sister's husband, Benjamin Buss, who brought a new and disturbing dimension to her life. Benjamin was a bit of a tearaway: he survived (as did many others in the area) by a bit of smuggling and the marketing of contraband, together with any other dubious money-making possibilities which presented themselves. But he was also young and good-looking and his cavalier attitude to the law and the establishment made him quite attractive to young Susannah. They became very close, the roguish Benjamin and the attractive Susannah, and even spent some brief visits to London in each other's company.

The less attractive and much older John Lott had not entirely given up his pursuit of the young damsel and he visited her in Rolvenden on several occasions, repeating his proposal of marriage. Susannah was repulsed by the idea, but the crafty Benjamin saw a possible opportunity to make some money out of the situation. John Lott was getting on in years and a young wife would have a very comfortable life and stood to inherit a considerable sum when her husband finally departed this life, which, given his advanced years, should not be too long in occurring. Obviously Benjamin anticipated sharing in his lover's good fortune, were she finally to agree to become Mrs Lott.

Susannah was not at all keen on the idea but Benjamin obviously used his undoubted charm and powers of persuasion and, reluctantly, she eventually agreed to the proposal, no doubt hoping that the marriage would not last too long.

And so, on Monday 15 August 1768, the couple were married at Rolvenden church. Despite the groom's wealth, the wedding was a very quiet affair, attended only by the couple, Susannah's sister and her husband, Thomas Buss, together with the ever-present Benjamin. After the ceremony they all repaired to the groom's house in Hythe to celebrate the nuptials.

It appears that, while at the 'reception' in Hythe, Benjamin became unwell and, according to Susannah's later statement, she made frequent trips upstairs to him and brought him various remedies for his unspecified malaise, all at her husband's express direction.

The whole wedding party passed the night in Lott's house but the next day Benjamin, apparently now a little better, began to press Susannah to hasten the day when she would inherit by plying her new husband with some toxic substance.

On the Wednesday, Thomas Buss and his wife returned home to Rolvenden, leaving Benjamin, still claiming indisposition, under the same roof as the newly-weds. This same day Benjamin repeated his proposal that Susannah should get rid of John Lott and, before they dined, he showed her a paper packet which, he claimed, contained some poison which he had obtained from the local apothecary's shop, where he had been served by an unsuspecting apprentice. He thrust this packet into Susannah's hand and repeated his suggestion that she administer the contents to her husband as soon as possible. Susannah, however, recoiled from the suggestion and threw the packet away.

After dinner that day all three went riding over some land which John Lott occupied and then stopped at a public house in Burmarsh where they called for a pint of milk bumbo (a mixture of rum, sugar and nutmeg in milk). While John attended to the horses and mended one of the bridles, the two lovers drank about half of the drink and, when John eventually joined them, he finished most of it off, remarking that it had a 'very hot taste' and that he had noticed something in the bottom of the vessel which looked like

The Shepherd and Crook, *Burmarsh, where the first dose of poison was administered to John Lott.*

paint. The landlady was proud of her bumbo and was concerned that Lott had criticized it as being unpalatable and so, after the visitors had left, she and her daughter tasted it and had to agree that it was possessed of a rather peculiar taste. However, they thought no more of it and threw the dregs of the drink away.

The unlikely trio continued their ride, during which Benjamin told Susannah that he had put poison in the half of the milk bumbo which John had drunk. The latter appeared at first not to have suffered any ill-effects, for they rode for around an hour and a half, before stopping at another public house in Eastbridge to drink tea. However, John Lott soon began to feel unwell, a fact which he put down to the milk bumbo, although he had no suspicion that it had been poisoned by Benjamin Buss. He repeated his earlier comment that it had tasted a little odd and rather hot, which he put down to pepper or something of that sort. To get rid of the unpleasant after-taste, he downed two dishes of tea, some brandy and water and a glass of gin. Not surprisingly, as they were leaving this hostelry, John was violently sick several times.

The newly-weds then made their way back to Hythe, by which time Benjamin had left them, expressing his intention of returning to Rolvenden. John seems to have been feeling a little better after his bout of nausea but stopped at another public house for more brandy on the way home.

During the night, however, the symptoms returned with a vengeance and John was violently sick and suffering from stomach pains and diarrhoea. First thing the next day, Susannah sent for an apothecary.

During that Thursday morning, Benjamin returned unexpectedly and asked Susannah if she had given her husband any more poison. She said she hadn't, adding that she had thrown it away. In a foul mood, Benjamin then left for Folkestone, returning later in the day with a bottle of white powder which he claimed was a poison. He again told her to administer this powder (later identified as corrosive sublimate or mercuric chloride) and she took the bottle, without actually agreeing to do as he wished or otherwise. In fact, once Benjamin had left the following (Friday) morning, she threw the bottle in the privy, or 'necessary' as she called it.

Benjamin returned the following Monday – just one week after the wedding – professing concern for the invalid but in reality checking to see whether the poison had been administered and taken effect. When he learned that it had been thrown away, he was furious and stormed off, not returning until the following Friday. By this time, the elderly John Lott was in a very poor state and he died that night while Benjamin was still in the house. Whether further poison had been administered is not known but, given Benjamin's resolute intention to do away with the old man, it seems highly possible.

On the Saturday morning, following the death of the unfortunate bridegroom during the night, Benjamin went off to Folkestone, where he apparently spent the night. He called in on the newly widowed Susannah on the Sunday, before returning to Rolvenden. This was the last time she was to see her lover and alleged accomplice in murder until after their arrest.

As might be expected, this sudden and, for the bride, fortuitous death was the subject of much speculation and suspicion. The fact that Benjamin had bought poison in both Hythe and Folkestone was disclosed, and the ladies at the public house confirmed that the bumbo they had served John Lott and his companions had indeed tasted odd. In fact, one of them was sick after tasting just a little of it.

The bereaved widow was brought in for questioning and was interviewed at length by Mr Tournay, the Town Clerk of Hythe, and she related to him much of what has been described above. He referred Susannah to the local magistrate, Mr William Deedes JP, who on the first day of September 1768, just two weeks after the wedding, extracted from her a full confession as to what had transpired. This was written out by the magistrate and Susannah, an uneducated young woman, affixed her 'mark' to it. Mr Deedes added a note to the effect that 'on being confronted by Benjamin Buss, the person now in custody, she declared him to be the person of whom she had related the above circumstances'. Susannah's confession having deeply implicated Benjamin, the justice of the peace had obviously wasted no time in issuing a warrant for his arrest and this had been diligently executed by the parish constable.

Hythe Town Hall.

Susannah was remanded in custody to Canterbury Gaol, where she languished for seven months before being transferred to the gaol in Maidstone. Here she spent a further four months until her appearance before the Kent Assizes. The reason for this unusual delay was the illness of the Hythe apothecary, Mr Gipps, who had been called as a vital witness for the prosecution. In the event he died before the case came to trial and so his testimony was never heard.

One unexpected result from this long period in prison before the trial was the arrival of a baby, born to Susannah in the gaol. She swore this was John Lott's offspring, insisting that she and Benjamin had never had any 'criminal conversation'. The production of this child for it to be breast-fed at least twice during the trial was no doubt intended to engender sympathy for the young mother, on trial for her life. A contemporary report remarked that 'her behaviour and lamentations over it after sentence had been passed would have forced tears from the most obdurate and insensible' (*The Gentleman's Magazine*, September 1769).

As for Benjamin Buss, when he was arrested he denied any knowledge of any crime committed against John Lott and he 'wondered why Mrs Lott should accuse him, who knew no more of the matter than the magistrate who committed him'. However, he too was remanded to prison, where he spent eleven months.

It was during this time in prison that Benjamin's bravado left him. He contracted the deadly gaol fever and, fearing he was about to die, he made a full confession, no doubt hoping to save his immortal soul. This confession tallied in every respect with that made by Susannah but, when Benjamin recovered from the fever, he promptly retracted it.

The trial of the two conspirators took place in Maidstone on 19 July 1769. Throughout the trial Susannah's comportment was modest and penitent, unlike that of Benjamin, who was described as 'impudent and obdurate'. He put on a great show of being the wrongly accused innocent in this matter, insisting that he had not been inside Lott's house from the time he was first taken ill until his death. However, this part of his story was quickly disproved by two witnesses who testified that he had slept in the house on the night Lott died.

Benjamin then introduced a woman who claimed that a contract of marriage existed between them, this evidently being a desperate attempt to distance himself from Susannah and to show that he had no interest in Lott's demise. This ploy too failed, as the court felt a man such as Benjamin would have no scruples about playing up to Susannah if he thought there might be some advantage for him and he would not hesitate to repudiate any contract if it suited him.

The hearing ended and there could be no doubt as to the outcome. Both Susannah Lott and Benjamin Buss were found guilty of the murder of John Lott by poisoning. Up until this point Benjamin had displayed an 'impudent indifference', but he now went ashen white and fell on his knees, begging for mercy.

But there was to be no mercy and the judge then pronounced sentence. Benjamin Buss was to be hanged and his body handed over to the surgeons for dissection. As for Susannah Lott, she was to be drawn on a hurdle to her place of execution and there be burnt until she was dead, the reason for this more extreme mode of execution being because the murder of a man by his wife was held to be petty treason. Indeed, not all that many years before, Susannah would have been boiled alive for such a heinous crime.

Just two days later, on Friday, 21 July 1769, the two convicted prisoners were taken from the old gaol in Maidstone to Penenden Heath, the traditional meeting place and place of execution for the county. Both were attired in black, Susannah wearing the mourning clothes she had bought for her husband's funeral.

At the Heath, Buss made a lengthy speech, admitting his guilt and acknowledging the justice of his sentence before he was finally 'turned off' as the actual execution was described in those days.

It was now Susannah's turn. Although the sentence called for her to be burnt to death, over the years the executioners had developed a more 'humane' system whereby the victim was first strangled so that she would not feel the flames as they licked around her body. Susannah was bundled to a large stake buried in the earth, some seven feet high. She was made to stand on a stool while they put a rope around her neck and attached it to a peg at the top of the stake. The stool was then kicked away and she was left to suffocate. After a quarter of an hour the dead or near-dead body was secured to the stake while faggots were piled around it. Once lit, the faggots burned fiercely and, in the words used at the time, 'she was soon reduced to ashes'.

Although prior to her death she was unknown outside the local area, the name of Susannah Lott was to become notorious as the last woman to be burnt at the stake in England.

Chapter 5

The Unfaithful Footman

C hislehurst is a village which today is within the London Borough of Bromley, but not so long ago (up until 1965) it was very definitely in the county of Kent. This was certainly the case in 1813 when our story begins.

Nowadays Chislehurst Golf Club, Camden Place is an imposing eighteenth-century manor built for the Earl Camden, one time Chief Justice and later Lord Chancellor. It is also the house where Emperor Napoleon III died in 1873, but in 1813 it was in the hands of the wealthy Mr Bonar and his wife who had lived there some eight or nine years.

Camden Place, where Mr and Mrs Bonar were murdered.

One Sunday evening in the early summer of 1813, Mr Bonar retired to bed at his usual time. His wife did not follow him until two o'clock in the morning, after ordering her servant to call her at seven. True to her instructions, the servant went to the master bedroom to wake her mistress. To her horror, she found the mangled body of Mr Bonar lying on the floor and her mistress, unconscious and dying, in her bed.

Mr Bonar's head and hands were covered with blood, his skull literally broken into fragments in several places. There was a great laceration across his face and nose as if caused by a heavy rod or bar. His hands were mangled and there was a severe wound to the right knee. From the injuries it was clear that Mr Bonar had put up a great struggle. Despite being in his seventies, he was a strong and fit man and sold his life dearly. His nightcap, lying a few feet from his head, was drenched in blood, with a lock of grey hair still adhering to it. His pillow, which had fallen from the bed, was lying at his feet; this too was drenched in blood.

His wife had had her head broken in the same manner but she seemed to have been knocked unconscious without a struggle, as her face displayed a calm softness, more as if she were asleep rather than dead or dying. Her bedlinen was soaked in blood, as was that on Mr Bonar's bed. Although the couple slept in separate small beds, these were placed so close together that there was scarcely room for anyone to walk between them.

A bent poker lying on the floor matched closely the injuries and wounds on the two bodies and was clearly the murder weapon. As there were still some signs of life in Mrs Bonar, Philip Nicholson, the footman, rode into London to fetch a surgeon, taking one of the best horses in the stables to ensure his speedy arrival. It is a measure of the Bonars' wealth and importance that they could afford the services of Mr Astley Cooper, who was the surgeon at Guy's Hospital, Professor at the Royal College of Surgeons and probably the most celebrated and important surgeon of his day. Mr Cooper attended without delay but it was too late: the injuries were too severe and the soul of Mrs Bonar joined that of her late husband at eleven minutes past one, her only utterance being a soft 'Oh dear!'

That evening Mr Bonar junior arrived from Faversham, where he was stationed as a colonel in the Kent Militia and, despite the efforts of friends and others to restrain him, rushed upstairs crying, 'Let me see my father. Indeed, I must see him!' He burst into the bedroom, locking the door behind him. Amid fears for his safety, the door was forced open and Colonel Bonar was found kneeling with clasped hands over the body of his father, apparently in prayer. His friends dragged him away, in a state of near collapse, into an adjoining room.

There appeared to be no explanation for this horrid and violent affair; there had been no attempt at robbery and it was hard to imagine anyone who would wish to commit such a bloody deed on two persons who were universally liked and respected for their inoffensiveness and benevolence. Strangely enough, the murder weapon was not thought to have been one of the household items and must have been brought in from elsewhere by the murderer. There were no signs of a break-in, although it was reported that the front door was found open in the morning. Only two hours after Mrs Bonar had retired to bed, a washerwoman let herself in to start work. None of the servants appeared to have been disturbed by any noise or cries during the night; their quarters were some distance from the master bedroom. Despite all the blood in the bedroom, there was no trace of a bloody footprint in the ante-room or the hall, and only one or two spots in the hall.

It was later revealed that once the footman had summoned the surgeon, he rode to the *Red Lion*, near Bedlam, where he saw a man named Dale, who had recently been discharged from the service of Mr Bonar, to whom it was later alleged he said, 'The deed is done and you are suspected. But you are not in it.'

Nicholson, the footman, then went on to Bow Street to inform the Bow Street Runners about the murders and he related what had passed when he saw Dale at the *Red Lion*. This prompted two officers to go in search of Dale. Nicholson appeared to be slightly tipsy and it is true he had been seen to down three glasses of rum at the public house. The officers told him to follow them but they lost sight of him in Brydges Street.

The officers found Dale and brought him before the magistrates at Bow Street for examination. It transpired that Dale had been employed by the Bonars as a butler but was discharged about a fortnight previously on suspicion of 'ill conduct'. It was said that Mrs Bonar wanted him to be prosecuted but her husband was content to dismiss him without references. The magistrates examined him closely but were content with the alibi he put forward, claiming to have been in the *Red Lion* from eleven on the Sunday evening until six o'clock the following morning, with several witnesses to support his claim (there was no law in those days to prevent drinking places from staying open all night if they wished). Dale was therefore told to go home to his wife in Chislehurst.

The funeral of the Bonars took place at Chislehurst church and was attended by a large congregation. A mournful cavalcade, including the undertakers, pages, mutes, and so on, moved slowly around the heath to the church, where the coffins were carried side by side to the grave.

With Dale being cleared of any involvement in the dreadful deed, suspicion fell on the footman, Philip Nicholson, and a warrant was issued by the Lord Mayor for his arrest. One of the Bow Street Runners immediately went in search of him and, on that same Monday, after a diligent search, the officer traced Nicholson to Whitechapel and found him, on horseback, drinking at the door of the *Three Nuns* alehouse. The officer grabbed the horse's bridle and, after a short scuffle, pulled the wanted man from his horse and took him off to Giltspur Street Compter, the debtors' prison near Newgate (demolished in 1855).

The prisoner was drunk and his demeanour was so bizarre that Mr Astley Cooper was called in to examine him. The surgeon was accompanied by Sir Charles Flower, the Lord Mayor of London, and together they asked the footman a number of questions but could not extract anything like a confession or admission of guilt. In view of his drunken state, Nicholson was remanded until the following day.

The next day, Tuesday, he was taken to the Mansion House, where he was again questioned. From the answers given to the questions put to him, his interrogators gained the impression that

Giltspur Street Compter, the debtors' prison near Newgate.

he had behaved in a most imprudent and unfeeling manner, which raised more suspicion than any other evidence available.

Nicholson said that, on the night in question, he went to bed about midnight and knew nothing until called by the housemaid about eight o'clock the next morning. He was the only male servant who slept in the house and he had fastened some of the windows himself at the usual time, the remainder being secured by the maid. With the discovery of the murders, all the servants gathered together and he, with others, went to the bedroom where he saw the two bodies, the floor being covered in blood and other matter. He took the bloody sheets off his master's bed and used them to mop up some of the mess on the floor and then took the soiled linen to his own bedroom, where the groom helped him to wrap it in the top sheet from his own bed. He then placed the bundle under his bed. He was questioned closely as to why he had used the sheets to absorb the blood and then fold them inside his own linen when he should have known that the proper thing to do was to leave everything undisturbed. Nicholson said he was unaware of this and had thought it his duty to tidy the scene as much as possible, as the sight would have been distressing to anyone entering the room. He was then asked about a bloody footprint found on the stairs leading from his room to that in which the murders were committed. He suggested that such a mark might have been made by him when he took the soiled sheets up to his room, but it was pointed out that the footprint was discovered before he first left his room.

In view of the struggle which Mr Bonar had obviously put up, Nicholson was stripped and examined in private but any bruises which were revealed could easily have been suffered in the scuffle with the arresting officer and when he fell from his horse.

Nicholson was then asked about his ride to town to seek the surgeon and admitted that he had left the house in Chislehurst shortly after eight o'clock and had stopped for refreshment for himself and the horse three times on the road. He had drunk three glasses of rum and the horse three pints of porter. Despite these stops, the surgeon confirmed that Nicholson had covered the whole distance in around forty minutes.

After notifying Mr Astley Cooper that his services were required at Camden Place to attend to the still-living Mrs Bonar, Nicholson said that he went on to the *Red Lion*, where he saw Dale and told him that he (Dale) was a suspect. He then continued to Bow Street to ask that an officer be sent down to Chislehurst. Nicholson was reprimanded at this point for having gone to find Dale who, had he been the culprit, would have been forewarned and could have absconded. He was also criticized for not having returned immediately to Camden Place but instead having gone carousing with friends, with whom he was still drinking when he was arrested. The interrogation complete, Nicholson was sent, in the charge of two officers, to Chislehurst to attend the inquest to be held there that evening.

The inquest opened promptly at six o'clock, the first witness being Mary Clarke, Mrs Bonar's maid. She told the jury that Mrs Bonar was in the habit of retiring late, usually around one or two o'clock in the morning, some two hours after her husband. She last saw Mr Bonar about ten o'clock that Sunday evening when he was reading prayers to his staff in the sitting room:

About twenty past midnight, I was summoned to Mrs Bonar's dressing room adjacent to the bedroom and I went there in my dressing gown. Mrs Bonar said she had ordered Nicholson, the footman, to secure the lawn door but he had failed to do so. I offered to go and do it but Mrs Bonar said that would not be necessary as she had locked the other door herself. I presumed she was referring to the folding door between the lawn door and the hall. I then undressed Mrs Bonar and warmed her bed, at which time I saw Mr Bonar asleep in his own bed nearby.

Mary returned to her own room to await the next summons and at about twenty minutes past one the bell rang again and Mary went to her mistress's dressing room and folded up her clothes, Mrs Bonar then being in the bedroom.

About fifteen minutes later, the bell rang again. Mrs Bonar was then in bed and I handed her the string which was attached to the door to enable it to be opened more or less.

Having been instructed to call her mistress at seven-thirty that morning, Mary lit the rush light in the ante-room and went to bed, leaving the doors of the bedroom and the ante-room both wide open, as was the custom.

At seven-thirty I was awakened by Susannah the housemaid as I had asked. The housemaid told me there was a bad smell in the ante-room, coming from the bedroom and asked whether I had lit the rush light as this was missing, and whether I had locked the door to the ante-room from the outside. She also said there were foot marks in the ante-room. I was much alarmed as these unusual circumstances led me to believe something dreadful had happened.

The pair went up to the ante-room to examine the marks, which they thought could be blood. Mary then went to fetch the laundry maid (who started her work at four o'clock) and they went together to the bedroom. The laundry maid went to the window and opened the shutters to let some light into the room. When she turned round her eyes fell on the terrible scene and she screamed. Mary fled the room and ran downstairs in a state of shock.

The coachman made me sit down as I was near to fainting and, whilst I was recovering, I saw the footman come into the servants' hall with a bundle of bloodied sheets. Philip Nicholson said to me, 'Mrs Clarke, go to your mistress, she is still alive and perhaps may be recovered.'

Susannah Curnick was the next witness. She had been the housemaid for only three weeks, all the other staff being in post before she arrived. On the night in question, she put the rush light in its usual place in the ante-room around ten o'clock and shortly afterwards went to bed.

I remember Mrs Clarke coming to bed and asking to be called at half-past seven. I myself rose at six-thirty and, on going through the hall, noticed that the house door was half open – something I had never seen before. I closed the door and went into the drawing room where all the windows were closed apart from the one in the centre which was wide open. On going upstairs I was surprised to find the door to the ante-room locked, with the key outside. I opened the door and noticed foot marks on the floor and that the rush light was missing from its stand.

Much perturbed by what she had seen, Susannah went back to the room she shared with Mary Clarke and told her what had occurred and together they went back to the ante-room. The rest of her story tallied with that told by Mary Clarke. On being questioned, Susannah said she had never heard the footman express any anger or disappointment towards her master. She had never noticed anything particular about his conduct.

Penelope Folds, the laundry maid, was the next to take the stand. She had been with the family for fifteen years, and that Monday morning:

I rose a little after four o'clock and was soon joined by Williams, the washerwoman, who let herself in by the laundry door. About seven-

thirty, Mary Clarke approached me and asked me to accompany her upstairs as she was afraid something was amiss. I did so and went into the bedroom and opened part of one of the shutters. When I turned round I saw the master's body lying on the floor and blood on the mistress's pillow.

She went downstairs but returned later and saw the footman covering Mr Bonar's body with a blanket and then meddling with the clothes on his bed and afterwards she saw the footman taking a bundle of soiled sheets downstairs. She found her mistress was still breathing and remarked that the footman was the first to say that Mrs Bonar was still alive. He said he must go to town for help although she asked him not to leave the house without a man in it.

William Evans, the groom, had been in the service of the family for the past few months:

I was in the house till after twelve o'clock on Sunday evening, sitting with the footman and I never saw him in a better humour. I have never heard him say anything disrespectful of his master or mistress, except now and then an angry expression at being overworked, such as 'the old woman, she wears me out!'

He added that he saw the footman dabbing the sheets in the blood at the foot of the bed. On being pressed on this point, he said that the housemaid, who was in the room at the time, could tell more about it.

Susannah Curnick was recalled and testified that she was never in the room at the same time as the footman, contrary to what the groom had deposed. She also said that the groom had exclaimed, at the foot of his mistress's bed, with a dreadful expression, 'This is what comes of keeping company with the Jews.'

William Randall had been coachman to the family for eight years and slept over the stables:

I came to the house about half-past seven and went to call Nicholson and found him sitting on his bed-side. Almost immediately I heard the cry of murder from the female servants. Not long afterwards I saw Nicholson come downstairs with bloody linen and wrap it up in a sheet in the servants' hall. The footman was a very quiet, good fellow-servant but, when he had money, he used to get drunk. The rest of the servants observed that they could not have handled the sheets as Nicholson did. He was very anxious to go to London and would have a horse. I thought Nicholson was wild looking when he went away and it appeared as if he could not ride, although he had been in the dragoons.

Charles King had worked for the family as a labourer for seven years and lived in Green Lane, Chislehurst:

I came to work at between five and six on Monday morning. I came to the house about twenty minutes after six. The washerwomen were up and so I got into the house by the laundry and went into the hall and found the front door open. Philip was then in bed and I said to him, 'How is it you sleep with the door and window shutters open?' He answered, 'I did not know that they were open.' I am sure he was in bed with his shirt on.

Mrs Williams, a washerwoman, testified that when she came to the house about four in the morning she noted that the hall windows were all open. Philip Shillington, the gardener, got up between three and four o'clock and he too noticed the middle drawing room window open, which he did not shut.

It was then Philip Nicholson's turn to take the stand. When asked what he had to state he replied, 'Nothing other than what I told the Lord Mayor. The windows of my bedroom were shut when I went to bed.' No further questions were put to him and he was released into the custody of a Bow Street officer called Lavender.

A Mr Smith stated that he came over on the morning of the murder and saw the bodies and the bent poker (modern police officers would be horrified at the failure to make any efforts to secure the crime scene):

I then went into the servants' hall and found a bundle which I opened. It consisted of two bloody sheets, one fine and the other coarse – which was the most bloody of the two. They were wrapped in a third. I gave the two bloody sheets to a servant called Sweetapple to take to Mr Bonar's room. A candlestick in Mr B's room was bent and broken. There was a small spot of white paint on the poker.

A reconstruction of the Bow Street Horse Patrol, which covered the outer parts of the capital.

Lavender, the Bow Street officer, stated that he arrived on the Monday about one o'clock:

> *I found a pair of shoes by the side of the footman's bed which I compared with the traces in the ante-room. As I thought, the impressions corresponded with the shoes which are not fellows. I found a night cap on the footman's bed, apparently bloody.*

Another witness, by the name of Foy, from Marlborough Street, compared the shoes which he had found on Tuesday morning in a closet in the servants' hall with the footprints and found that they tallied:

> *The shoes were odd; one common heeled and worn at the toe, the other with a spring heel, as was the case with the shoes which Lavender found. There was blood on both the soles and on the uppers. I showed them to Nicholson who agreed that they were his. He said he believed one of them had slipped off in the room from which he fetched the sheets, but I found them together in the cupboard. Nicholson also told me that the stains on his night cap probably came from the blood on the sheets.*

The poker was then produced. It was a common kitchen poker, about 2 feet 4 inches long and bent in the upper part.

The inquest closed at one o'clock the next morning, with the jury returning a verdict of wilful murder against Philip Nicholson, the footman. It seemed clear, from the blood on it, that he had disguised himself in one of the sheets from his own bed when he went to murder his employers but, fortunately for the prosecution, he left the sheet in the room, which accounted for his anxiety to get the bloody sheets out of his master's room – one (the fine one) from the victim's bed and the other (the coarse one) the one he used to cover himself when he went to perform the terrible deed.

The accused was confined to the butler's pantry, in the care of two Bow Street officers, awaiting escort to London but, at noon that day, the court was informed that the assassin had cut his own throat with a razor he had found in the butler's pantry and concealed about his person. He had been permitted to use the lavatory in the passage leading to the servants' hall, where he had used the implement to try to take his own life. However, although the wound was deep and bled profusely, there happened to be two surgeons nearby who had attended the inquest, and one of them, Mr Holt, immediately rushed forward and seized the gushing arteries with both hands and contrived to stop the flow with manual pressure until more regular means could be applied and the wound sewn up.

By that evening Nicholson was out of immediate danger and was able to speak but he said very little and made no confession or explanation, merely protesting his innocence. To prevent any further attempts to take his own life, Nicholson was put in a straitjacket and his arms were held by two persons, one on each side of him. His head was also held steady to prevent him from opening up the wound. A Bow Street officer and servants were always in the room to watch him.

On 7 June 1813 he received numerous visitors, mostly highly placed friends of the murdered couple, including Lord Castlereagh the foreign secretary, Lord Camden and Lord Robert Seymour, and was showing repeated signs of annoyance and agitation. Eventually, that evening, the wound opened up again and Nicholson bled profusely. All this time he had persisted in asserting his innocence, but early the following morning he asked that Mr Bonar junior be brought to his bedside. When the heir to the Bonar fortune arrived, Nicholson broke down and confessed to the crime and made a full signed confession to a local magistrate. At last the true story came out.

On that fateful Sunday night, after the groom had left him, Nicholson fell asleep on a bench in the servants' hall. Around three o'clock, he fell off the bench and awoke and was instantly seized with the idea of murdering his employers. He was already half-undressed and so he wrapped himself in a sheet from his bed and took the poker from the grate in the servants' hall and a lighted candle and made his way upstairs.

I went directly to my mistress's bed and struck her two blows on the head. She neither spoke nor moved. I then went round to my master and struck him once across the face. Mr Bonar was roused and, from the confusion produced by the violence of the blow, imagined that Mrs Bonar was then coming to bed and said, 'Come to bed, my love.' I immediately repeated the blows and he sprang out of bed and grappled with me for fifteen minutes and at one time nearly got the better of me but, being exhausted by the loss of blood, I at length overpowered him.

Nicholson then left his victim groaning on the floor and went downstairs, where he stripped naked and washed himself all over in the butler's pantry. He then opened the drawing room windows to make it look as if there had been an intruder. He disposed of his bloodied shirt and stockings in a bush outside the front door, covering them with leaves. He then returned, leaving the front door open and went back to bed. He did not sleep but pretended to be asleep when King came to wake him at six-thirty.

Nicholson completed his deposition by emphasizing that he was alone in this deed and had no associates. 'How could I, when never in my life, before the moment of jumping up from the bench, had I entertained the thought of murder?'

A search by the officer, Lavender, quickly revealed the soiled garments Nicholson had concealed and he was sent for trial at the Maidstone Assizes before Mr Justice Heath on a charge of petty treason. This indictment differed from a common indictment for murder in that the victim was the offender's master and he therefore traitorously as well as feloniously murdered his master. (This distinction was removed in 1861.) Nicholson pleaded not guilty.

Nicholson's confession was read out and, asked what his motive was, he replied, 'I had no bad intention. I did not know what provoked me to do it, more than you do.'

'You were heard to complain about going so much behind the carriage.'

'Yes, but I never thought of doing it from that.'

'Had you thought or talked of this murder when you were drinking with the groom the night before in the hall?'

'No. I never thought of it myself, or had any idea of it myself.'

'How long was it after you awoke that you went upstairs?'

'I jumped up. I was half undressed when sleeping on the form. I undressed and put the sheet about me.'

'Why did you put the sheet about you?'

'That they might not know me.'

'When did you drop the sheet?'

'In the struggle. I had it on when I gave the first blow.'

'Did Dale the butler or any of the maid servants know anything about it?'

'Not a word.'

'What was your intention?'

'Nothing particular, but when I went into the room I saw my master and mistress asleep and I gave her two blows.'

'Were you drunk when you went to bed?'

'No Sir. I had drunk nothing but beer. I had not had a drop of spirits all day.'

After examination and the evidence provided by witnesses for the prosecution, a Mr Frederick Tyrrell appeared as a character witness. He told the court that Nicholson had been employed by his father but had been ultimately dismissed for drunkenness, although the witness said he was never violent.

The judge summed up the evidence, saying he had never known a case more clearly proved. The jury immediately returned a verdict of guilty and the judge, after a protracted homily, continued,

> I shall therefore proceed to discharge my duty in passing upon you the sentence of the law, which is that you be taken hence to a place from whence you came, and on Monday next be drawn on a sledge to the place of execution, and there hanged till you are dead, and then your body shall be given to be dissected and anatomized.

Nicholson was therefore taken to the condemned cell at the old Maidstone Gaol (this was well before the present prison was erected) which was underground and approached by a dark and dreary staircase.

Around midday the following Monday, the hurdle or sledge, in the shape of a shallow box about 6 feet by 3 feet, drew up at the door to the gaol. It had a seat at each end, just capable of holding two persons and Nicholson was placed in it with his back to the horses with the executioner seated beside him. Facing them were the priest and a gaoler with a loaded blunderbuss on his lap.

The contraption made its way slowly the mile and a half to Penenden Heath, where a platform about 7 feet high had been erected with the gallows on top. Mr Bonar junior was already there in a post-chaise, facing the place of execution, determined to witness the dispatch of his parents' murderer. He did not have long to wait, for very soon the trap was sprung and Nicholson was launched into eternity. As was not uncommon in those days, the execution was carried out without any semblance of scientific or biological finesse and, according to contemporary records, 'he died unusually hard, being greatly convulsed'.

Chapter 6

The Nine-Shilling Murder

R obert Taylor was a semi-invalid, former tallow-chandler, who lived in Strood, near Rochester, and now worked as a general labourer. Because of his impecunious circumstances and disability, he received a weekly allowance of nine shillings from the parish of Aylesford where he used to live and, on Friday, 4 March 1831, as was his custom, he dispatched his 13-year-old son, Richard Faulkner Taylor, to Aylesford to collect this allowance as he was not able to make the journey himself.

Young Richard was described as having unusual intelligence and an amiable disposition; he was dressed at the time in a canvas 'southwester', with a belcher handkerchief round his neck, a blue jacket and waistcoat, brown trousers, and shoes and stockings. At Richard's particular request, his father lent him a knife, with which he expressed his intention to cut a bow and arrow on his way home. The boy had previously been instructed by his father as to how he should carry the money, and Richard had shown him how completely and securely he could conceal it by putting it into a little bag, which he could carry in the palm of his hand inside a glove which the boy wore.

It was Richard's usual practice to take his 7-year-old sister with him on these expeditions but, on this occasion, she was not ready and, expressing his impatience, he set off without her, leaving Strood between nine and ten that morning. On the way he met up with Warrant Officer Lewington of HMS *Warrior*, who accompanied him to the top of Blue Bell Hill where they parted ways, Richard descending the hill towards Aylesford.

About one o'clock Mr Lewington again saw Richard, this time in the company of two boys named Bell, the sons of a labourer who was then working on grubbing root vegetables on the Common below the *Blue Bell* public house. The Bells were a near-destitute

The brothers James and John Any Bird Bell.

family who lived in the poorhouse in Crow Lane, Rochester. The three boys were later seen again, heading towards Rochester, by Mrs Mary Jones, who lived at Bridge Wood Cottage, between the pub and the turnpike gate. The boys unsuccessfully asked the gatekeeper for some water, after which the younger of the two Bell boys, James, went off on his own. They returned home later that evening separately, James being the first to arrive.

Richard usually reached home at about three o'clock but this afternoon he failed to return. It grew dark and, as the night advanced, the boy's father became more and more concerned at his absence. As soon as it was daylight the next morning he set off to make enquiries and learned that Richard had arrived safely at Aylesford, where Mr Cutbath, the assistant parish relieving officer, had given him the usual nine shillings allowance. Sure enough, on this occasion he had been seen to conceal the coins in his mitten as described above.

A search was made but proved unavailing, and the boy's parents were left to dread what might be the cause of his sudden disappearance. The Bells, father and two sons, were taken into custody and questioned but said they were unable to explain what had happened to young Richard. John Tuff, the Rochester parish constable (later to be the officer in charge of the Rochester City Police, although these events occurred six years before that force was formed), went to various places to try to trace the boy, assuming he was still alive and living elsewhere. In all, the constable travelled more than two hundred miles in his fruitless search and, in April, took the three Bells – father and sons – and two other men to make a thorough search of the woods beside the Maidstone to Rochester road. Despite working close together in as straight a line as possible, ignoring all obstacles in their way until the clothes were nearly torn from their backs, they found nothing, although it later transpired they had passed within 5 yards of Richard Taylor's body. The two boys were in very high spirits and amused themselves by robbing birds' nests throughout the search.

It was not until some two months later, on 11 May, that the true circumstances were discovered. That morning, a farm labourer named John Izard was going to inspect a stack of sainfoin (a plant used as fodder) when he took the wrong path through Great Delce Wood some two miles from Rochester and found the body of the boy lying in a ditch around 150 yards from the main road. The mitten had been cut from his left hand, and his clothes were disarranged, as if there had been a scuffle.

The horrified John Izard continued on his route to the farmer's field, where he asked two men working on the road to come with him as he believed he had found the missing boy. One of the men, James Taylor from Chatham, knew the boy and confirmed Izard's suspicions. The men then went to notify Constable Tuff and the boy's father, who promptly attended the scene.

The body was so decomposed that the constable was unable to discover the cause of death, but traces of blood on the shirt, coat and neckerchief left no doubt as to the dreadful death which the boy had suffered. Subsequent examination revealed that his throat had been cut with a sharp-pointed instrument – a wound he could not possibly have inflicted on himself.

An inquest was held on 13 May, in the course of which the younger of the two Bell boys, James, aged twelve, was questioned by the coroner and said,

I knew Richard Taylor as I had often seen him on his way to Aylesford. We played together in Summerfield's turnip field on the day he disappeared. Richard showed me the money in his hand and asked if there was nine shillings there. I counted three half-crowns, a shilling and a sixpence and said there was nine shillings. Richard put the money back in a little bag in his glove and said he must be off as his father had nothing to eat and his mother had promised him three farthings. My brother was with us but he didn't see the money. Richard had a knife in his hand but I didn't have one. He then went through the field into the lane where there are houses.

The elder of the two Bell boys, John Any Bird Bell, aged fourteen, also said he knew Richard by sight and they were together in Mr Summerfield's turnip field, where Richard had a knife.

I didn't have a knife but my brother did. We each took a turnip and my brother cut his with his shut knife. Richard left us just after one o'clock and me and my brother played about after he had gone and got home about five o'clock. I didn't see any money but my brother told me he had nine shillings safe in his glove. Richard said he should cut a walking stick but he must make haste as his father was coming to meet him.

This discrepancy concerning the possession of a knife by the Bell brothers led to James being recalled.

Me and my brother didn't get any turnips. Taylor took one. I didn't have a knife. Taylor had his father's knife. Me and my brother got a turnip each after the other boy had gone and I peeled mine with my teeth and John did the same. I don't think he had a knife. He did carry a knife sometimes but it is now at home.

John responded:

My brother peeled his turnip with a shut knife. He generally carries a knife. I had no knife, I picked the dirt off with my fingers. My brother had a knife.

James answered that he did not think he had a knife with him on that day.

John Bell senior, the father of the two boys, stated that he saw the deceased boy going up Blue Bell Hill:

The old Blue Bell Hill. The main road has now been diverted and made into a busy dual carriageway, but the old road still exists beside it.

My boys were with him. They were going to get some greens from Mr Summerfield's turnip field. I told them to get them. I returned home about seven o'clock and didn't see the boys again until then. My boy sometimes carries a knife. They didn't bring any turnips home. I know nothing of the murder.

Robert Taylor, the father of the deceased boy, confirmed that he had sent Richard to collect his allowance:

Mr Burch allowed him to ride as far as Kit's Coty House [a prehistoric megalith] *where he turned off to go to Aylesford. He had been several times before to receive the money. I was very much alarmed when he did not return. I made all the enquiries I could about him and searched the neighbourhood but I could not find him. I heard nothing more of him until John Izard came and told me. I went to the woods and recognized the body as that of my son. I stayed as long as my constitution would admit but not until the body was removed. Before the boy left the house, he asked me for my knife. I lent it to him and gave him a penny to buy a cake. I told him I would meet him if I was better but my legs took to swelling and I was unable to go.*

Kit's Coty House. The prehistoric megalith mentioned by Richard Taylor's father in his statement.

Mr Edward Seaton, the parish surgeon, had examined the body at the poorhouse and found it to be in a very decomposed state.

> *The windpipe or trachea was entire, with the exception of one spot where it appears to have been cut into with some cutting instrument. ... A part of one of the muscles of the neck had escaped decomposition and appeared to have been divided by a sharp instrument. ... It is my opinion that he died of a consequence of a wound made on the left side of his neck by some cutting instrument.*

Mr Seaton's findings and opinion were confirmed by another surgeon, Mr Jacob Bryant from Chatham, and the Coroner's jury returned a verdict of 'Wilful murder against some person or persons unknown'.

The day following the inquest, Saturday 14 May 1831, the two Bell boys were taken into custody and interrogated by two magistrates over six days without any success, despite another witness stating that he came across three boys answering the description of those concerned as he came down Blue Bell Hill. One of the boys was being assailed by the other two and so he turned his horse and rode part of the way back up the hill to give the victim some protection. When he returned shortly afterwards there was no sign of the assailants. Later on, this witness identified the two Bell boys as the assailants.

Perhaps worn down by the unremitting questioning, on the next day, Saturday 21 May, James Bell asked to speak to one of the magistrates, the Reverend Davies, alone and told him that the previous evening his brother had told him that he had murdered the little Taylor boy with his own (Taylor's) knife. On being confronted with this betrayal (which James later admitted was an invention), John Any Bird Bell confessed to the murder. A full judicial inquiry was commenced by a panel of six justices, during which the depositions of those who had given evidence before the Coroner were taken and further witnesses gave their testimony.

Warrant Officer Henry Lewington said that, when he heard that the body had been found, he went from the *Blue Bell* public house to where Bell and his sons were at work and took them into custody. He brought them back to the pub, where the older boy sat apart from the other two and did not speak.

John Bell, the father of the boys, was called next and told that he was being held in custody on a charge of being an accessory before or after the fact of murder. He denied any knowledge of the crime, either before or after it was committed. On a later occasion, Bell admitted that he was not married to the woman with whom he now lived and who was the mother of the two boys. He had other children by a previous marriage, the eldest of whom was now more than twenty.

At this point, it was decided to open up the grave of the dead boy (he had been buried immediately after the discovery of his body and the Coroner's inquest, still wearing the clothes in which he had been found), so as to obtain the knife which his father had lent him and the glove and so confirm the statement made by John Any Bird Bell. A Mr James Dadd was sent to open the grave and Constable

The 'Countless Stones' referred to by James Bell.

Pattison took the Bell boys with him in order to observe the effect this might have on them. John maintained a sullen silence throughout but, on being asked to enter the grave and search the body, young James cheerfully complied, and was helped down into the pit. The boy quickly brought forth the knife and glove from the breeches pocket of the putrid corpse and was helped out again. There being no money in the glove or elsewhere on the body, it could now be assumed that robbery was the motive for the killing.

With the evidence now amassed and the confession by John Any Bird Bell, the magistrates continued with the committal proceedings, starting with James Bell, who was duly sworn in. He related that, on the day in question, he and his brother had been sent on an errand by their father but took their time in accomplishing it. They were searching for peas among some discarded stalks when Richard passed them, after which they tried to count the 'Countless Stones' – a heap of large stones reputed to be the remains of a rude Druidical altar. A little later John took James's knife and sharpened it on a sandstone. He kept the knife in his hands as he had no pockets.

The knife was then produced by Constable Pattison, who stated that he had taken it from another youth, Henry Perrin. James identified the knife as his and went on to say that when they reached the Kit's Coty field they saw Richard Taylor returning up the Aylesford Road. He soon caught up with them and they walked on together until they reached the place where John Bell senior was working. The two younger boys lay down on the bank and it was here that the conversation about the nine shillings took place. After a while, John came up with two pieces of bread and they all went off up the hill together. They passed the *Blue Bell* and went through a gate into the wood, where James asked his brother, 'Are you going to do it here?' To which John replied, 'Yes.'

In fact, the trio continued across the main turnpike road to go in search of some turnips to eat. John and Richard went into a turnip field while James waited outside by the road for a while and then made his leisurely way home. This was the last time he saw Richard.

James had already told John about the nine shillings and John had said, 'I shan't give you half.' To which James replied, 'Two shillings will do.' However, when the boys met up again outside their home, John offered James one and sixpence, which he refused. After some discussion, John returned James's knife to him and gave him half a crown, which he accepted. He was later to have great difficulty in changing this quite large sum for more convenient coins, but eventually spent one shilling in local shops and put three sixpences aside.

Although he had been repeatedly cautioned not to say anything, John Bird interjected at this point, 'He said one shilling would do for what I should do the crime.'

James continued to carry and use the knife which had been used to kill Richard for some time thereafter. He later sold it to Henry Perrin for ninepence, insisting that the sale was for the money and not because of the use to which it had been put previously.

Constable Pattison gave evidence, stating that on the first occasion that he had escorted John Any Bird Bell to Maidstone Gaol, where he was to be detained pending further examination, the prisoner acknowledged the truth of his brother's statement, and pointed out a pond where he had washed the blood of his victim off his hands and knife on his way home after the murder. He also pointed to the opening in the hedge which led to the spot where the body was found and said to the officer: 'That's the way to the place where I killed the poor boy.' Then he added: 'He is better off than me now: do not you think he is, sir?'

The young prisoner proved quite talkative on the journey to Maidstone and described to the constable how, while they were in the wood, he had told Taylor that they were lost, whereupon the boy threw himself down and burst into tears. Seizing his opportunity, John leaped on the unfortunate lad and cut his throat. He then forced the money bag from Richard's tightly clenched hand. 'I know I shall be hanged but I hope James will be able to come and see me so that it might be a warning to him to behave better in future.'

Having heard the evidence of these and other witnesses, the magistrates committed the two boys for trial on a charge of murder, the chairman, the Reverend A Browne, castigating their parents, especially the mother, for the way they had brought the children up:

> *The manner in which they have been brought up has rendered them so hardened as to excite almost the surprise and indignation of every person who has seen the way in which they have behaved themselves during their examination. They have had no sense of feeling whatsoever as to the situation in which they have stood. ... They have been taken into schools where every attention has been paid to their morals, but their conduct has been so bad at those schools that, for fear of contaminating the other children, they have been dismissed from them. ... You* [to the mother] *said that you never knew them guilty of any act of stealing but it has been brought home to you that you have frequently known it – that you offered money at one time to compromise a matter, to prevent your boys getting into trouble.*

At eight o'clock on Friday 29 July 1831, John Any Bird Bell, aged fourteen, appeared at the Maidstone Assizes on a charge of having feloniously, wilfully and of malice aforethought, killed and murdered one Richard Faulkner Taylor, in the parish of St Margaret in the County of Kent on 4 March 1831. The prisoner pleaded not guilty. Every available seat in the courtroom had been occupied well before this time, such was the interest in this case.

Evidence was given by the victim's father Robert Taylor, Mr Cutbath the Assistant Overseer at Aylesford, Warrant Officer Henry Lewington, Mary Jones, John Izard, the surgeons Edward Seaton and Jacob Bryant and Constable John Tuff.

Mr George Furrell, the Clerk at the practice of Messrs Twopeny and Essell, solicitors and Clerks to the Justices, described how he wrote down a statement, amounting to a confession, made by the prisoner. He explained that he had been taking down a statement by the prisoner's brother, James, when John began to speak. The clerk immediately stopped taking the statement from James and started to write down what the prisoner was saying, although he spoke so fast that the clerk had difficulty in doing so. The prisoner was repeatedly warned that anything he said would be used against him.

The admissibility of this statement was very closely challenged by the defending counsel but Mr Justice Gazelee, after consulting a brother judge, ruled that, although the manner in which the confession was taken and recorded was grossly irregular, it was not necessarily a fatal error.

The confession made by the prisoner, John Any Bird Bell, was therefore read out in court:

> *Going down to Abbott's my brother says 'there goes Taylor down – let's kill him and take his money and let's lay him under them stones what you can't count over twice.' He lent me his knife – sold that to Henry Perrin. … It was me, sir, that done the murder, sir – in the wood sir. … We went along the wood and could not find our way out; then he lay down and cried … and then I cut his throat as he lay. I had no great difficulty to cut his throat – did it at one cut –'twas done in one cut. That's the frock I had on (pointing to a blue frock then worn by his brother James); nobody has washed it since. I took the nine shillings out of his glove. My brother said if I didn't give him half he'd tell. … He said before I did it he only wanted a shilling, but after I'd done it he wanted part and I gave him one of the three half-crowns. He squeaked, sir, that's all – not much – as a rabbit squeaks. I'm fourteen or fifteen years old. I gave the knife to James the same night. I washed it and my hands in a pond on the road. There was no blood on it when I gave it back to my brother.*

Other witnesses for the prosecution gave evidence, identical to that which they had given at the inquest, after which the case for the prosecution was closed. The prisoner said he had nothing to say and that he had no witnesses. Asked by the judge if he wanted to call anyone who knew him, Bell replied, looking round the court, 'My mother is somewhere in Maidstone.' Evidently his mother did not think it necessary for her to be present at the trial of her son on a capital charge.

After the judge had summed up, the jury remained in their box and took but a few minutes to return a guilty verdict. However, they made a recommendation for mercy on the grounds of the prisoner's 'extreme youth and the profligate and unnatural manner in which he had been brought up'.

Mr Clarkson, the defence counsel, made a plea for a stay of judgement on the grounds of the admissibility of the confession but the judge ruled that he must pronounce judgement in the usual manner. Placing the black cap on his head, the judge then addressed the boy at some length, saying that, although he would pay every attention to the jury's humane recommendation, he was afraid he could not give way to such feelings but must cause the death sentence to be executed. Since the prisoner was obviously sane and was well aware of the consequences of his actions, he could not hold out the slightest hope of mercy.

The sentence which I have to pronounce and which will leave no hope that the execution will be stayed, is that you be taken to the place from whence you came and on Monday next to the place of execution; that you be hanged by the neck till you are dead; that your body be dissected and anatomized according to the statute, and may the Lord have mercy on your soul.

At the trial the young prisoner had exhibited the utmost indifference to his fate, and appeared to have no fear of the consequences of his guilt. He remained steadfast throughout the judge's address and the sentence of death, but exhibited some emotion when he was informed that part of the sentence was that his body should be given over to the surgeons to be dissected.

And so, John Any Bird Bell, a month or so short of his fifteenth birthday, became the first victim to be executed on the moveable long drop erected for the occasion at the entrance lodge to the new Maidstone Gaol. Expecting the execution to take place at eight o'clock, a large crowd had gathered outside the gaol by that time on the morning of Monday 1 August 1831. By eleven o'clock, when the prison bell began to toll, the crowd had grown to not less than six thousand, many of them females, to watch the spectacle. The boy was brought out from the condemned cell and, on seeing the assembly awaiting his arrival, said in a low voice, 'Pray for a poor boy! Pray for me.'

He then cried out, 'All you people take warning by me – take warning!' as the trap opened and he fell to his death.

Despite their father being a poor but apparently literate and honest worker, a regular churchgoer and possessing high moral standards, the two young boys, and John in particular, were already addicted to crime. John had stolen horsehair, a number of clasp knives (including the murder weapon), committed thefts from shops by breaking windows and had undoubtedly been concerned in the robbery of the Maidstone coach just before it entered Rochester. It seems clear that his mother was much too complacent about the boys' misdeeds and, by her actions, undid much of their father's attempts to instil some discipline and standards into his progeny, with the dreadful result described above.

Chapter 7

Away with the Fairies

Most of the killers whose deeds are described in this book suffered the ultimate penalty – death – which was the only permitted sentence until the middle of the twentieth century. However, a few escaped execution for one reason or another and did not end their life on the gallows at Penenden Heath or, later, at Maidstone Prison.

Richard Dadd was one of these. Born on 1 August 1817 in Chatham, he was the fourth of seven children of comfortably well-off, artistic parents. So comfortable, in fact, that they were able to pay for him to attend the King's School in Rochester, an independent choir school, nestling against the ancient cathedral. At this distinguished educational establishment – the second oldest in the world, being founded in 604 and later restored and given royal patronage by King Henry VIII (hence its name) – he developed a taste for the classics in general and Shakespeare in particular. He left this school in 1834, at the age of seventeen, when the family moved to London, where the father took up work as a carver and bronzeworker in the Haymarket.

Unlike most young men of his age, Dadd seems to have had no need to work for his living but showed considerable promise as a painter, being admitted to the august Royal Academy at the remarkably young age of twenty. His style of painting followed the so-called 'Fairy School', which reflected his passion for Shakespeare, especially works such as *A Midsummer Night's Dream*. The Victorians were obsessed with fairy tales – even Sir Arthur Conan Doyle was prepared to authenticate the now infamous Cottingly fairy pictures, which were later found to be an elaborate photographic hoax.

In his early twenties Richard Dadd found a patron in Sir Thomas Phillips, a lawyer and former mayor of Newport in South Wales

Richard Dadd at work.

who was knighted for his part in putting down a Chartist riot, in the course of which he was shot and seriously wounded. Phillips decided that Richard would benefit from a Grand Tour, as undertaken at that time by most men of quality or those who, like him, had a powerful and rich patron. And so in 1842 the pair set off on their travels and adventures, visiting various parts of Europe before heading for the Middle East.

Dadd seems to have enjoyed the travels, although he complained that the constant displacements gave him little time for painting, but it was while they were in the Middle East that Sir Thomas began to detect signs that all was not well with Richard Dadd's mental state. It is known that Dadd took part in an extended smoking session with some Arabs he met in Egypt, allegedly spending five whole days using the 'hubble-bubble' water pipe or 'hookah', after which he began to suffer from headaches. He became obsessed by Egyptian mythology, and was devoted to the god Osiris.

His behaviour became more and more erratic and, by the time the travellers had reached Italy, Dadd was suffering from paranoid delusions of pursuit and became increasingly violent towards other people, including Phillips. While in Rome Dadd experienced an uncontrollable urge to attack the Pope on one of his public appearances and was dissuaded only with difficulty. His companion put this behaviour down to sunstroke but, by the time the pair reached Paris in the spring of 1843, the younger man's violent behaviour could no longer be ascribed to the effects of the sun and Dadd was returned to England.

Back home, Dadd's family sought specialist medical advice, and Alexander Sutherland, a consultant psychiatrist from St Luke's Hospital, declared Dadd to be non compos mentis, or of legally unsound mind. Instead of having him committed to an institution – which would certainly have been the case had the subject not been of Dadd's social and financial standing – the doctor advised that he should be allowed to rest and suggested they move from London to the country, where Richard could recuperate.

And so Richard and his father went to spend some time in the village of Cobham, just a few miles from Richard's birthplace at Chatham (and later to be a favourite haunt of Charles Dickens). Here Richard said he would 'disburden his mind' to his father. Just how he proposed to do this is not known, but Dadd's father was prepared to try anything which might save his son's sanity.

On the evening of 28 August 1843, after dinner in the inn where

'Dadd's Hole', where Dadd senior was killed. The pit has now been largely filled in.

they were staying, the two men, father and son, went for a walk in the warm summer air, smoking their postprandial cigars and chatting amiably together. Their route took them by a chalk pit called Paddock Hole (now known as 'Dadd's Hole') not far from their lodgings, and it was here that Richard Dadd finally succumbed to his mental devils. Without warning, he suddenly took a razor from his pocket and slashed his father's throat. The older man fell gurgling to the ground, where his life soon left him. Completely untroubled by his deed, Richard then produced a knife from his pocket and set about dismembering the still-warm body. Eventually, leaving his father's mutilated body where it was, lying in the undergrowth, Richard left the blood-soaked scene.

Early the next morning Abraham Lyster, a Rochester butcher on his way to work, discovered the ghastly, dismembered body of

The Ship Inn *at Cobham, where the body was taken and where the father and son probably stayed.*

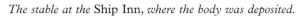

The stable at the Ship Inn, *where the body was deposited.*

Dadd senior lying beside the chalk pit. At first he thought it was merely a tramp or a drunk sleeping off an excess of alcohol but he noticed the clothing was that of a gentleman so he went to investigate. Turning the body over, he saw the ghastly wounds and so ran for help. The local constable attended the blood-soaked scene with a surgeon, but there was nothing the latter could do for the victim.

An examination of the body revealed that Dadd's gold watch was still in his pocket, as were three sovereigns, so it was not a matter of robbery. The wounds and the position of the body ruled out the possibility of suicide and so it was concluded that it was the work of a madman. With the identity of the dead man as yet unknown, the body was removed to the *Ship Inn* in Cobham where a waiter recognized it as being that of a man who had taken tea there the previous day in the company of a rather strange young man. As a result of this information, the identity of the dead man was soon discovered, as well as that of his son.

There was no sign of Richard and the authorities began a frantic search for him, at first fearing that he too could have been murdered by the same maniac.

Richard's brother in London was informed of the death of his father and, knowing his brother's mental history, immediately became suspicious and told the police of his concerns. Officers from the Metropolitan Police searched Richard Dadd's apartment, where they found a number of disquieting paintings and drawings. Many of these were of Richard's friends and acquaintances and all were depicted as having had their throats cut. And so, much too late, the hunt was on for Richard Dadd, not as a victim but as a crazed killer.

Meanwhile, still wearing his bloodstained clothing, Richard Dadd had somehow made his way to Dover, stopping off briefly at the *Crown Inn* in Rochester, where he at last washed the blood from his hands. On reaching Dover he boarded a boat for France and not until he arrived in Calais did Dadd finally change out of his bloodstained clothes before setting off for Paris. Not content with his recent foul act of patricide, once in the French capital he attempted to cut the throat of a fellow tourist while travelling in a coach near Fontainebleau. Fortunately the astonished victim, a complete stranger, was able to fight off his attacker and escaped with comparatively minor injuries. The French police were called and arrested the would-be assassin, whereupon Dadd told them his name and confessed to the murder of his father. He was taken to the local *commissariat de police* where he was placed in a custody cell or *garde à vue*, pending the magistrate's instructions, later being moved to a French lunatic asylum. It was while he was detained in this asylum that a list was found concealed upon his person, giving the names of people who, according to his deranged mind 'must die'. His father's name headed the list.

After nearly a year of detention in France, Richard Dadd was extradited to England in July 1844. On his arrival he was immediately charged with the murder of his father and brought before the magistrates in Rochester. The hearing was a complete pantomime, with Dadd constantly interrupting the proceedings and mimicking the magistrates. He frequently burst into irrational outpourings, such as, 'I tell you I didn't do it; no gammon about it; no, I shan't do it; I dare say, I can say; I shan't do that; I never did it I tell you; oh gammon; I know sir.'

He was eventually remanded in custody to appear at the Kent Assizes, where he was subsequently tried for the crime. His insanity was, however, quite obvious by this stage and so the McNaghten Rules were applied and he escaped the gallows, being instead committed to the Bethlem Hospital or, as it was more familiarly known, 'Bedlam', in Bishopsgate.

In the asylum, Richard Dadd was in due course diagnosed as having what is now known as bipolar manic depression. He was encouraged to continue painting and did so with great enthusiasm, producing some of his finest works of art. His masterpiece is generally thought to be *Fairy Feller's Master-Stroke*, which he took nine years to complete (although he personally never considered it as having been finished). The painting is literally three-dimensional, so thick are the layers of paint which Dadd carefully applied. He worked obsessively in minute detail, using a magnifying glass for some of the more minuscule parts. The original painting is now in the Tate Gallery, where it is displayed

Richard Dadd's masterpiece, The Fairy Feller's Master-Stroke.

using a raking light, the better to highlight the three-dimensional qualities. Like many of Dadd's later works, one needs to study them for several hours in order to appreciate the subtleties of this madman's art.

In July 1864, possibly due to the overcrowding at Bedlam, Richard Dadd was removed to the new lunatic asylum at Broadmoor – later to become the asylum for the criminally insane – where he remained until his death, from natural causes, in January 1866.

Chapter 8

A Soldier and his Lass

I n 1856 the short-lived but bloody Crimean War came to an end and the troops began to return home. Most of these belonged to long-established British regiments, but there were also some curious military formations, such as the British German Legion, the British Italian Legion and the British Swiss Legion. It was only recently that the latter had been secretly created at Dover – secretly because it was in flagrant contravention of Swiss law, under which mercenary service in foreign armies was strictly prohibited.

On its return from Russia, the Second Regiment of the British Swiss Legion was stationed at Shorncliffe Barracks, just outside Folkestone, awaiting demobilization or a further posting. Among this raggle-taggle of European mercenaries was a small, slight, somewhat sickly young man by the name of Dedea Redaines. He was not Swiss, having been born in Belgrade, Serbia, but this was not unusual as all sorts of nationalities were to be found in these rapidly formed 'Legions'. Desperate for manpower (or perhaps more correctly 'cannon-fodder') the British government was not particular whom it enlisted and volunteers were welcomed with open arms and no questions asked.

One of Redaines's tasks was to take the Legion's laundry to a washerwoman in Dover where, despite his somewhat unprepossessing appearance and limited command of the English language, he managed to find himself a girlfriend in one of the washerwoman's daughters. The young lady in question, Caroline Back, around eighteen years of age, lived with her parents and younger sister, Maria, in Albion Place, Dover. The young Redaines quickly became besotted and it seems that she returned his affection and, to quote from contemporary records, they 'contracted an intimacy'.

As a result of this liaison, Caroline eventually told Redaines that she was pregnant with his child but Redaines was a jealous young man and suspected his sweetheart of carrying on with someone else. For some reason, he believed she was two-timing him with one of his sergeants, for there was a certain sergeant in the Legion who had met Caroline and Redaines believed that he had been paying court to her and that his advances were not entirely unwelcome.

One fine summer's Friday in early August 1856, Redaines made one of his regular trips to Caroline's home and asked her to come to Shorncliffe with him 'to meet his sister' who, he said, had recently arrived there. Caroline was delighted to have the chance to meet up with a member of her boyfriend's family from abroad as this was tantamount to an engagement. She excitedly sought her parents' approval but Mrs Back was not entirely sure of the propriety of such a proposal. However, in view of Caroline's heartfelt entreaties, she agreed to the venture on condition that 16-year-old Maria accompanied them, presumably as a chaperone. Accordingly, the trio set out at 3 am the next morning to walk the ten miles from Dover to Shorncliffe. It was apparently Redaines's intention to confront Caroline with his suspicions of her infidelity during the long walk in the summer dawn.

This little party, making its way along the coast road towards Hougham in the early morning light, was observed by Constable Herd of the Dover Borough Police. He recognized Redaines, as he had previously been in custody in Dover for an assault on police. It seems therefore that, despite his small and slight stature, the little Serbian had something of a temper and a disposition towards violence.

Around 5 am the trio were seen passing a public house on the outskirts of Capel-le-Ferne, some three and a half miles from Dover and still a long way from Shorncliffe. Perhaps their slow progress was a result of an argument between Redaines and Caroline but this we shall never know since, as the little party neared a secluded spot known as Steddy Hole, near the *Valiant Sailor* public house on the main Dover to Folkestone road, Redaines suddenly struck. Plucking from his belt a dagger he had

Members of one of the British Foreign Legions of the type in which Dedea Redaines served during the Crimean War.

bought the previous day in Dover, he plunged it once, twice, thrice, four times into Maria's breast. She had no chance to resist or to fight off her attacker and, within minutes, her lifeless body was lying on the grass at his feet. Despite her complete innocence and her lack of involvement in the love affair between the couple, young Maria was the first to die.

Caroline, walking a few paces ahead, turned just in time to see her sister brutally struck down. Horrified, she realized it would be her turn next as Redaines ran at her, with blood lust in his eyes, the bloodstained stiletto raised ready to strike. Caroline was not going to surrender her life without a fight, however, and the lacerations found on her arms and hands were ample testimony to the

Steddy Hole, overlooking the Warren near Folkestone, where the double murder was committed.

The Valiant Sailor *public house close to Steddy Hole.*

desperate struggle she put up. But despite his small stature, Redaines was wiry and strong and eventually the knife found its mark and Caroline's body joined that of her sister. Like Maria, Caroline had suffered four separate wounds to her chest, piercing her young heart.

Around 8 am, Caroline's body and that of her sister were discovered by a passing farm worker. No real effort had been made to hide the bodies and both the girls' cloaks were missing, as of course, was Dedea Redaines.

Despite the primitive means of communication available in mid-nineteenth-century rural Kent, the alarm was quickly raised and news of the ghastly affair soon spread throughout the area. Since there was no sign of Redaines, he was obviously the prime suspect and a general hue and cry was raised during the rest of that fateful Saturday and over the next couple of days.

Efforts to organize a widespread search were considerably hampered by the lack of a rural constabulary. Although there were now regular police forces in towns such as Dover and Folkestone, the countryside was still policed, as it had been for the best part of a thousand years, by part-time, unpaid and often unwilling parish constables. And so, despite the efforts of an outraged public, there was no sign of Redaines until between 4 and 5 pm on the following Monday, when some workers at Lower Hardres, near Canterbury, were startled by the sudden appearance of a wild-looking creature, coming across the fields, wearing a girl's cape and carrying another. Despite the fact that this was some fifteen miles from the scene of the crime as the crow flies – and a lot further through the winding and twisting country lanes of rural Kent – the men instantly realized that this was the man sought by the authorities for the terrible double murder two days earlier. Faced with these angry but understandably rather nervous labourers who had armed themselves with whatever suitable agricultural implements they could lay their hands on, Redaines realized that the game was up and, producing the stiletto, stabbed himself in the chest three times. Heartened by this, the men closed in and secured the injured fugitive, and took him into Canterbury and handed him over to the city police force.

In view of his injuries, Redaines was first taken to the Canterbury hospital where, because of his limited English, he was interviewed by Dr Rhost, a linguist from St Augustine's College. The good doctor was unable to make much sense of Redaines's explanations, which simply amounted to the fact that he had done it for love.

In due course Dedea Redaines recovered from his self-inflicted injuries and was taken into custody to await his trial, which took place at the Kent Winter Assize in Maidstone towards the end of 1856.

At no time did Redaines deny killing the two girls and, on being arraigned, pleaded guilty to the murder of Caroline Back but not guilty to that of her sister, Maria. He appeared to be bewildered by having so many charges of murder levelled against him. In the light of his plea the trial went ahead on the charge of the murder of Maria, since his guilt on the other charge had been admitted.

The hearing was not a long one and the jury took but a few minutes to return a unanimous verdict of guilty of the wilful murder of Maria Back on 2 August 1856. Given that Redaines had already pleaded guilty to the murder of Caroline, the judge simply had to pronounce the sentence which, by law, could only be that of death. Accordingly, the judge solemnly placed the piece of black cloth on top of his full-bottomed wig and sentenced Dedea Redaines 'to be hanged by the neck until he was dead'.

Following his conviction he was placed in the condemned cell, where he appeared to be perfectly composed. Father Lawrence, the local priest, who spoke some German, was convinced that Redaines was insane but his opinion was not enough to save the young soldier. William Calcraft, the rather clumsy public executioner, was called for and, on the very first day of the year 1857, went to the condemned cell, where he pinioned Redaines's hands (a new procedure) and led him to the scaffold which had been specially erected outside Maidstone Prison. After a few suitable words from the chaplain, Calcraft sprang the trap and the Serbian went to meet his Maker.

Contemporary newspapers report that a considerable number of people witnessed the execution but 'behaved in an orderly and decorous manner'.

Redaines's body hung on the scaffold for the prescribed hour to ensure that life was extinct, after which he was cut down and the scaffold dismantled. By a macabre coincidence, one of the workmen dismantling the timber structure had the misfortune to fall from a considerable height onto his head and died immediately – the second death on that spot within little more than an hour.

Chapter 9

The Turning of the Worms

Many murders and violent attacks are premeditated and carried out for personal gain or to get rid of an inconvenient spouse or lover. Others, however, are the result of a simmering sense of injustice or of bullying tactics exercised by the ultimate victim, who is usually someone in a position of power or authority. Two such cases took place within the space of a decade in nineteenth-century Kent.

In 1856 the Crimean War was over and the troops were returning to Britain, in some cases bringing with them problems which had their origins in that far-off land. Private Thomas Mansell was one such soldier. He was one of a number of troops encamped in Hospital Meadows at Hougham, just outside Dover. He had performed his duties well and bravely in the Crimea and was prepared to settle down to the life of drill parades and exercises

British troops during the Crimean War, where Private Thomas Mansell served. From a painting by Lady Butler.

which were to be the lot of most soldiers in peacetime England.

Mansell had one big bugbear, however: his immediate superior was Lance Corporal Alexander McBurney and there was a long history of personality problems between the two. It seemed clear to Mansell that McBurney was determined to get him into trouble one day or another.

The matter came to a head one fine summer's day in August 1856 when Mansell picked up his kitbag under the watchful eye of the corporal. On searching through the kitbag, Mansell found, to his astonishment, that his own, new boots were missing and, instead, there was a pair of well-worn boots which McBurney instantly claimed as his own, accusing Mansell of having stolen them. In response, Mansell accused the corporal of having placed his boots in the kitbag and having removed his (Mansell's) own footwear, with the sole intention of getting Mansell into trouble. McBurney denied this and told Mansell he would be on a charge and up before the commanding officer in the morning. It must be remembered that flogging was still the punishment for many breaches of the Army Regulations at this time, especially the theft of a comrade's kit and, it being a question of one man's word against another, the senior of the two was more likely to be believed. Private Mansell was incandescent with rage and fear for what the morrow might bring.

Mansell went to his tent but was unable to sleep with the worry of the impending disciplinary action. He tossed and turned in his cot and finally, in the wee small hours, got up and, picking up his rifle, went to Lance Corporal McBurney's tent. McBurney was still up, cleaning his equipment, no doubt with the intention of creating a good impression before the commanding officer next morning. He looked up when Mansell entered the tent, which McBurney shared with other soldiers, and was concerned to see the intent expression on Mansell's face and the rifle in his hands. Mansell immediately raised the weapon and pointed it at his tormentor but another soldier passed between them when he was about to fire. A matter of seconds later the target was unobstructed and, from a distance of just 3 yards, Mansell fired, the bullet hitting McBurney in the side.

The other soldiers in the tent, horrified at what they had just witnessed, grabbed Mansell, who put up no resistance. The wounded lance corporal was transported to the hospital in Dover where he died almost immediately.

The matter was now outside military discipline and Mansell was handed over to the civil authorities to deal with this cold-blooded murder. Accordingly, in October 1856, Private Mansell appeared before the Kent Assizes in Maidstone, where he admitted he could not positively say that the deceased soldier had swapped the boots with the intention of getting him into trouble because of their long history of mutual animosity. It was, as he put it in a letter to a comrade, 'a case of great excitement and irritation'. He told the court that he was extremely sorry for the crime which he had committed but that he could not avoid it for, that morning, he was worked up to a pitch of madness. 'I hardly knew what I had done.'

Mansell's defence counsel astutely latched onto this testimony by his client and put forward a strong plea of insanity: 'Who in their right mind would contemplate committing such a murder, in front of a whole regiment, unless he was completely deranged?'

But the plea was rejected and the jury quickly returned a verdict of guilty of the murder of Lance Corporal Alexander McBurney with malice aforethought. There could only be one sentence and Private Thomas Mansell was ordered to be hanged for his crime.

The defence was not finished, however, and lodged an appeal to have the sentence set aside on a writ of error. Despite protracted proceedings in the Court of Appeal, the application was finally rejected seven months after the conviction and, on 6 July 1857 Private Mansell was hanged by William Calcraft before a comparatively small crowd outside Maidstone Prison.

At Thomas Mansell's wish, his Crimea campaign medal was handed over to his regiment.

The summer of 1856 in Dover appears to have been quite a heated one – whatever the weather conditions were at the time – since, as we have just seen, it was also in August of that year that another soldier, Dedea Redaines, murdered his girlfriend a matter of a mile or two away from the scene of this later incident.

★★★

Convicts in Chatham Prison.

The second murder referred to at the beginning of this chapter occurred some ten years later, this time not involving a soldier but a convicted prisoner in the old Chatham Prison.

James Fletcher, a remarkably fine-looking young man of twenty years of age, was serving a sentence of seven years' penal servitude, indicating a long criminal history for one so young. He was also obviously prone to violence: in the course of one particular period of labour, Fletcher got into a dispute with another prisoner and verbally threatened him, using some very strong language.

Fletcher was accordingly reported by James Boyle, a warder at the prison, for using abusive and bad language to another prisoner. For this misdemeanour the governor ordered that he should be given two days' solitary confinement on bread and water.

Fletcher was released from his lonely cell on 5 September 1866 and set to work breaking stones, supervised by Warder Boyle. Still smarting over his punishment and the fact that the other convict had not been disciplined, Fletcher deliberated how he might get his own back on the warder. After the lunch break he made up his mind what he would do and kept an eye on the prison clock. Every fifteen minutes he told himself, 'I'll do it in another quarter of an hour.' For three hours he worked sullenly and silently, turning his plan over and over in his mind. At four o'clock there was a short rest break and, looking at the clock, this time he decided he would not wait another quarter of an hour but would do the deed then and there. Accordingly, he suddenly rose from his seat and rushed across to where Warder Boyle was seated and struck him three times in the face with the hammer he had been using to break the stones. Such was the force of the blows, the victim's nose and all the bones in his face were smashed, leaving a hole completely exposing his brain. There was no way James Boyle could survive such injuries and his death occurred very swiftly.

One of the armed guards rushed across and seized Fletcher, wounding him slightly with his bayonet in the process, whereupon Fletcher dropped the hammer and surrendered without a struggle. He was handed over to Superintendent Everist of the Rochester Division of the Kent County Constabulary to be dealt with for this vicious assault.

At his trial at the Kent Assizes for the wilful murder of James Boyle, Fletcher claimed he had been provoked by the conditions in the prison. He recited a long list of complaints in mitigation for the crime, including the small meals of poor quality, unjust punishments imposed and other, generally trivial, complaints, none of which were substantiated. So far as the actual assault was concerned, he maintained that Boyle should not have reported him without reporting the other convict he was arguing with and it was the injustice of his subsequent punishment which prompted him to wreak his revenge on the officer.

Not surprisingly, none of these ramblings cut any ice with the court, which no doubt felt that prison life was meant to be harsh and a deterrent. After a short trial, Fletcher was convicted and sentenced to be hanged, whereupon he turned extremely violent and had to be put under restraint in order to be conveyed to the condemned cell in Maidstone Prison.

Justice was remarkably swift in those days and so it was that, at noon on 10 January 1867, a mere four months from the date the crime was committed, James Fletcher was hanged outside Maidstone Prison. The county authorities, no doubt in the interests of efficiency and economy, decided that Fletcher should be executed at the same time as Anne Lawrence (see Chapter 13) and so he had the dubious distinction of being involved in a rare double hanging.

William Calcraft was commissioned to perform the two executions together, which meant he had only one journey to be paid for and the same scaffold could be used for both hangings, all valuable considerations as far as the authorities were concerned.

James Fletcher was the first to be led out of the condemned cell, followed by Anne Lawrence, and they both stood on the trap door together, a noose around each of their necks. One pull on the lever and the trapdoor opened, dropping both to their deaths at once.

This exceptional 'two for the price of one' execution took place before a large crowd of onlookers who had gathered outside the gaol, all anxious to take full advantage of the unusual and free 'entertainment' being offered them.

Chapter 10

The Killer Died Happy

Robert Alexander Burton was a rather intelligent and good-looking 18-year-old who lived in Chatham in the mid-nineteenth century. Originally apprenticed to a carpenter, it was not long before he decided he wanted to join the forces. A few years earlier he could have enlisted in the army and gone to fight in the Crimea but all was now peaceful and neither the Army nor the Royal Navy was seeking recruits, and so this opportunity was denied him. Nevertheless, he managed to join the West Kent Militia (a forerunner of the Territorial Army), from which he promptly deserted with his bounty money. He next worked for a shoemaker, from whom he stole, and received a two-month prison sentence – all before his eighteenth birthday.

Whether any of these experiences affected his mind we shall never know, but it is clear he developed a strange fixation: he wanted to die. But not for him the ignominy of suicide: he wanted to go out with a bang, if not in some heroic military action, at least in a blaze of notoriety. No, the only answer was to kill someone and so be hanged for murder.

But whom to kill? His first choice would have been Mr Clark, the shoemaker for whom he had previously worked, who had preferred charges against him, resulting in the prison sentence. But Mr Clark had left the town and was therefore out of reach. The next possibility was the landlady of a certain public house in Chatham who had refused to serve him on some occasion (he was obviously a lad who harboured grudges). However, he felt this would be too much of a public affair and he might be prevented from carrying out his nefarious intention by customers in the pub or other onlookers. No, he first needed to hone his killing skills on someone in a more private place before returning to settle his score with the lady publican.

He was not a particularly robust or sturdy young man and so he quickly decided against murdering a male victim, who might well resist and perhaps even overpower him. It had to be a woman, or perhaps a boy.

He was still pondering on the matter and brooding on life's general unfairness when, one fine July day in 1862, he saw Mrs Houghton walking with her 9-year-old son, Thomas Frederick, in Chatham High Street. Burton knew the couple by sight and followed them for a short distance until Thomas left his mother's side and went off on his own. At this point Burton saw his opportunity and began to hatch a plan. He soon caught up with the boy who, since he knew Burton by sight, was not particularly alarmed. Burton chatted amiably with him as they strolled along and then, by some subterfuge or other, enticed the boy into the rather desolate area known as the Great Lines. This place, which lies behind and to the north of Chatham High Street, is still to this day largely undeveloped but in the nineteenth century it was a particularly wild area, given over to military sports and manoeuvres.

Once he was sure they were out of sight of any curious onlookers, Burton suddenly attacked the boy, stabbing him in the throat with his pocket knife. With a strangled cry, the lad fell to the ground, whereupon Burton trod heavily on his face and neck and, when this failed to bring about the poor unfortunate Thomas's demise, knelt on his stomach and put his hands around his throat. 'I pressed until the blood gushed from his nose and mouth,' Burton later admitted. With life having finally left the wretched victim, Burton calmly got to his feet, left the scene and went home, making no attempt to hide the boy's body. On the way he called at the *Dark Sun* public house and disposed of the murder weapon by tucking it under the eaves of the privy there.

Despite the remoteness of the Great Lines, it was not long before Thomas's body was discovered and a great outcry was raised. Who could have committed such a dastardly deed? There were no witnesses to the crime and few if any clues at the scene to assist the police. Given the lack of any relationship or connection between the killer and his victim, it is unlikely that Burton would have been caught had he not been determined to take credit for his actions.

The next evening, with the investigation at its height, Burton decided it was time to confess and get his brief period of glory. The obvious thing would be to go to the nearest police station, but the

A general view of the Great Lines at Chatham.

A further view of the Great Lines, showing the heavy undergrowth around the perimeter of the extensive military training ground.

Kent County Constabulary had only been formed five years earlier and the authorities had not yet got round to building police stations (the 'new' police station at the junction of New Road and Old Road would not be built for a further two years).

The man in charge of the new 'Rochester' division of the County Constabulary was Superintendent Thomas Everist and, with no police station, he had no alternative but to work from his home in Alma Terrace. He was used to this, having been responsible for the policing of Chatham for the past twelve years – even before his present appointment on the formation of the County Constabulary. Burton undoubtedly knew where Superintendent Everist lived and so, late in the evening of 24 July 1862, he set off for Alma Terrace, but on the way he stopped at the police stables where he saw Constable Stephen Hibburd, the superintendent's groom who, even at this late hour, was busy working there.

Without a moment's hesitation, Burton went up to him and boldly claimed, 'I murdered that boy on the Lines.' Hibburd was in two minds as to whether this was a hoax, a prank, or whether the claim was real. However, he was not prepared to take a chance and promptly took Burton into custody and marched him off to the superintendent's house.

On the way, Burton chatted freely to his captor and described exactly what he had done to Thomas Houghton. As they approached Alma Terrace, Burton realized that this was also where the mother of the dead boy lived and became rather agitated and asked the constable, 'You are not taking me to the boy's mother, are you?'

To his relief, the constable stopped at Superintendent Everist's house, just four doors away from where the dead boy's mother lived, where he handed the prisoner over to his superior.

After a few searching questions, the two policemen and the self-confessed murderer went to the scene. There, the constable enquired on which side of the neck the boy had been stabbed, and the superintendent told him it was the left. Burton immediately interjected 'No sir, it ain't indeed; if you look you'll find it's on the right side, just here,' indicating the place on his own neck. 'I only stabbed him once.'

If this valuable piece of information did not completely convince the officers that Burton was indeed the killer, his next offer to show them where the knife was hidden would have clinched the matter. Burton led them to the pub, where he retrieved the pocket knife.

On the way, Burton chatted with the two policemen, saying,

I had not any particular ill-feeling against the boy but I made my mind up to kill somebody. I know the boy and know where he lived and I know his mother and where she lived.

There was blood on Burton's clothing and, given his confession, his guilt was clear. All that remained was for him to be tried for this wanton and senseless crime.

For one reason or another it was not until the following spring that Burton appeared before the Kent Assizes. When asked how he pleaded, he responded with a smile, 'I am guilty.' However, on the judge's advice, the plea was changed to one of not guilty so that a full trial could be held and all the facts disclosed. An attempt by defending counsel to plead insanity was rejected and Burton was tried for murder.

There could only be one verdict and one penalty. Burton was found guilty of the murder of young Thomas Houghton and sentenced to be hanged. During the trial he displayed the utmost indifference, laughing most of the time and, when the sentence was finally pronounced, put a finger to his forehead and said, 'Thank you, my lord.'

In the brief period between the sentence and the execution, Burton wrote to Mrs Houghton and asked for her forgiveness which, with great generosity of spirit, she gave. 'Now I can die happy!' he said.

On 11 April 1863, the public executioner, William Calcraft, brought Robert Alexander Burton to the scaffold which had been erected outside Maidstone Prison, slipped the hempen noose over his head and dispatched him to eternity. Such was the notoriety and repugnance with which this senseless crime was viewed by the public, that the execution was witnessed by a crowd estimated at between 6,000 and 8,000 people. And Robert Burton achieved his ambition to be hanged, a notorious killer whose deeds would be remembered long after his lifeless body was removed from the scaffold.

Chapter 11

Deluded or Insane

There have been a number of mass murderers over the years and also many cases of the murder of unwanted infants but there can have been few cases quite like that of Stephen Forwood.

Forwood was a baker by trade and lived and worked in the seaside town of Ramsgate. He married a local girl, Emily Sarah Frances, whose family set him up in his own bakery business. However, the marital relationship was not a smooth one, partly because of Forwood's infidelities but mainly because of continual money problems, probably aggravated by gambling, and the business failed after only a little more than a year of marriage.

Stephen Forwood later confessed to running up debts of £1,800 – a huge sum in those days – and, in an attempt to resolve his financial problems and avoid detection by his creditors and possibly the police, Forwood left the marital home early in 1857 after yet another row with his young wife, neither of whom, it would seem, was aware that she was pregnant at the time.

Stephen Forwood made his way to London where he worked as a journeyman baker and, later, a travelling rope salesman. It was fast becoming obvious that, not only was he a disastrous businessman, he was also possessed of a turbulent and restless nature. From London he travelled to Bristol, from where it seems he intended to emigrate to America, but he evidently changed his mind and moved instead to Bath. It was during this period that he became seduced by the billiard halls, which were becoming very popular and offered endless opportunities for gambling. He discovered that he had a natural talent for the game and, by this means, he was able to eke out a precarious living. In May 1857 he went to live in Liverpool before moving on to Dublin and then to Glasgow, each stage being lower down the social and economic scale, until he was reduced to living on the streets and begging for food.

By 1862 he was in Brighton, where there were plenty of opportunities to win money on the billiard tables. He was determined to win back at least the £1,800 he still owed (and for which he could be thrown into a debtors' prison) and so redeem himself. That winter, while walking near the seafront, he encountered a young woman who, although of genteel manners, was desperate and contemplating suicide. Mrs White was the young mother of three children, married to a schoolteacher who had abandoned her and the children. She was running ever deeper into debt, and suicide seemed the only solution.

Forwood became enamoured of this sad lady and eventually entered into a relationship with her, setting up home with her and her three children. In the fullness of time another infant was added to the brood, of which he was the father. He seems to have been genuinely fond of all the children, both his new companion's and his own youngster, and acted as father to them all, irrespective of their parenthood.

With his own debts now augmented by those of his paramour, Forwood found it hard going to build up any capital, but his luck was to change. In February 1863 he won the princely sum of £1,172 from the Honourable Dudley Ward, an inveterate but penniless gambler. In the past, Ward's elder brother, the Earl of Dudley, had settled his gambling debts in order to protect the family name, and Forwood was therefore told to apply to the Earl for payment. But the noble lord had had enough and, deciding that his brother must learn to stand on his own two feet, declined to meet any more of his gambling debts.

Forwood returned to travelling around the country in search of work or other ways to gain money. With Mrs White he moved to Surbiton and then to Worcester, mostly living on his successes at billiards. He continued to send letters to the Earl of Dudley, seeking payment of the gambling debt, but without success. He even sent Mrs White to the Earl's house in an endeavour to extract the money, but she was simply thrown out.

By August 1864 the family were living in Putney, from where

Forwood wrote endless and voluminous letters to prominent people, such as the Bishop of London. He also began stalking the Earl of Dudley, turning up everywhere the Earl went.

With growing financial problems and the demands of his new family, Forwood became more and more despondent and desperate. He was later to claim that he had 'utterly worn out every power' in his efforts to find a home, some education and a little money for the children. Even his attempt to gain admission for the family in a refuge had been denied him. 'My sufferings were no longer supportable,' he complained.

After a fruitless trip to France on the tail of Dudley Ward, Forwood returned home to find that Mrs White had left with the apparent intention of sailing for Australia to start a new life for herself and her family. She had not yet taken the children with her but had left them with their father, William White. Forwood went to William White's abode in Holborn and managed to convince him that he would be sailing to Australia with White's wife and children, and the father released the children into Forwood's care. In fact, Forwood only took the children as far as a nearby coffee house.

The previous day, Saturday, 5 August 1865, Stephen Forwood had gone to the *Star Coffee House* in Red Lion Street, where he enquired if three children could be accommodated for a few nights. He was told that there would be rooms free for the children, aged six, eight and ten years of age and so, on the following Monday evening, having collected them from their father's custody, he returned with Mrs White's three children and saw them to bed in their rooms above the coffee house.

At half-past eight on the Wednesday morning, one of the chambermaids went into one of the two rooms occupied by the children and found the two younger ones dead in bed. She immediately raised the alarm and, when the proprietor and others entered the room where the older child had been placed, they found that he too was dead.

Medical assistance and the police were sent for, the surgeon being the first to arrive. He quickly determined that the children had been dead for some hours, rigor mortis having set in. From some bottles left in the room, the doctor deduced that they had all three been killed by poisoning with prussic acid the previous night (Tuesday). The police made their enquiries and established that the children had been brought to the inn by a man who gave the name of Southey – an alias which Forwood was now using in order to avoid his creditors – and the next day a search was mounted for him, since there seemed little doubt that he was responsible.

Why had he done such a terrible deed? It seems that business failure, mounting debts and an inability to provide for Mrs White and her family were now compounded by Mrs White's apparent intention to go to Australia without him. Rejection was now being added to his years of failure.

His description having been circulated by the Metropolitan Police, in order to avoid being recognized, Forwood, alias Southey, donned a false beard and green spectacles and made his way to Ramsgate, even though he had had no contact with his wife there since he left eight years previously.

Emily Sarah Forwood, his true wife, was in dire straits, having been left wholly unsupported by her lawful husband throughout this time. She had managed to scratch a living, for herself and the child (also called Emily), whom Stephen Forwood had never seen, by doing a little dressmaking, supplemented by the parish relief.

On arrival in Ramsgate, Stephen Forwood went to the King Street home of a dyer called Mr Ellis with whom he was acquainted. At Forwood's request, Mr Ellis went to where Emily Sarah Forwood was then living and arranged for her to come to his house to meet her estranged husband, on neutral ground as it were.

The meeting was not a calm and restrained one. As can well be appreciated, the main subject of discussion was money, or rather the lack of it. Emily Sarah Forwood was furious that she had been left all this time without a penny of maintenance for her or her daughter. For his part, Stephen Forwood was totally obsessed with his own problems, including the fact that he was to all intents and purposes destitute. Tempers were so inflamed that it was decided to adjourn the meeting until the next day.

At eight o'clock sharp the next morning, Emily Sarah Forwood went with her daughter Emily to the Ellises' house, where her husband was waiting for her. In an apparent attempt to lay down the ground rules for the meeting, his first comment was, 'Mind, last

George Ellis's home at 77 King Street, Ramsgate, where Forwood murdered his wife and child. The ground floor is now part of a carpet retailer's premises and the upper floors are no longer inhabited.

night I had nothing but reproofs; I don't want any more of it.'

Mr Ellis then said to little Emily, barely seven years of age, 'Do you know that gentleman?', indicating Forwood. Emily had, of course, never met her father and so replied quite honestly, 'No.'

'Go and ask him who he is,' pursued Mr Ellis, which she did. Forwood looked at the child intently and then, to his wife said softly, 'Is this ours?'

'Indeed it is,' she replied, and Forwood bent and kissed the child tenderly.

Emily Sarah Forwood was still beside herself with anger. 'Why have you come back here if you have no money for me? What do you want from me?' Forwood offered to explain himself to her but, looking at Mr Ellis, said, 'It is a private matter.'

Mr Ellis took the hint and went to his workshop, while his daughter suggested that the couple continue their personal discussions in the upstairs sitting room, where they could sort out their problems in private. They accepted the suggestion and went upstairs, still arguing, and were later followed by their daughter.

Shortly afterwards, the sound of two shots were heard and Mr Ellis rushed back into the house. With his daughter, he bounded up the stairs where, to his horror, he saw little Emily's body lying on the landing, outside the sitting room. He burst into the room where he saw Forwood standing there, a pistol in his hand and a blank look on his face.

'Forwood,' he cried, 'What have you been doing?' Forwood made no reply and, on being asked to do so, silently handed over the pistol to Mr Ellis. Looking round, the latter then saw the body of Emily Sarah Forwood, blood oozing from a wound to her head.

'Why have you done this?' he asked.

'She has seen a great deal of trouble and so have I,' said Forwood in reply. 'She is better off than ever she was but as for me, when I return to London I shall be under sentence of death for what I have left behind. It is better that she is dead for if she had not been, she must have heard of my being sentenced to death in London.'

Forwood was obviously anticipating his fate because, of course, at this time he had not been arrested for the London murders, let alone tried and sentenced to death. Perhaps now resigned to the inevitable, Forwood then removed the false beard and glasses and threw them in the fireplace.

Mr Ellis called out to his daughter to send for a surgeon and the police. Forwood added, 'Yes, send for a policeman.'

A messenger was dispatched to the police station house, which was then located at the town hall (the first Ramsgate police station in Charlotte Place was not established until nearly a decade later), and the head of the Ramsgate Borough Police attended the scene in person. Although Superintendent Livick had held the post for some twenty years and had a long policing career behind him, it is unlikely that he had ever encountered such a scene as that which awaited him in this modest Ramsgate dwelling. Nevertheless, he quickly took charge of the situation, arrested Forwood and took him back to the station house. At noon the same day, Forwood appeared before the local magistrates, charged with the two murders. Before any witnesses were called, Forwood confessed to the murders of the three children in London, the news of which had by now reached Ramsgate. In the light of this confession and the fact that Forwood answered the description of the wanted man, Superintendent Livick told him that he would also be charged with the murder of the three children in Red Lion Street, Holborn.

Forwood then elected to write a statement regarding the London murders:

On Monday the seventh, I took three children whom I claim as mine by the strongest ties to … Holborn … I had utterly worn out … every power … in my efforts to secure a home, training and a fortune for these children and also for the other five [sic] persons I felt hopelessly dependent upon me … My sufferings were no longer supportable. My very last hope had perished by my bitter and painful experience of our present iniquitously defective social justice, and for this I shall be charged with murder – for criminal matters as well – in the truest, strongest sense of the charge. I deny and repudiate the charge and charge it back on many who have by their gross and criminal neglect, brought about this sad and fearful crisis.

The long and rambling statement went on to lay the blame on the Church, the State and Justice, all of which he claimed had refused his pleas for assistance. At no time did he deny any of the murders, in London or in Ramsgate, and merely continued to insist that there had been no alternative and that the victims were better off dead.

Stephen Forwood, thirty-five years of age, appeared at the Kent Winter Assize in Maidstone in December 1865, charged with the murder of his wife, Emily Sarah Frances Forwood and her daughter, Emily.

To begin with, Stephen Forwood objected to being addressed by that name and asked that his name be altered to Ernest Walter Southey, claiming this to be his more usual name, although no reasons were given as to why this should be so. However, the judge agreed and, the charge being read out to him, he was asked if he wished to plead guilty or not guilty. He refused to answer and asked to be allowed to address the court before pleading but this breach of court procedure was refused by the judge, Mr Justice Mellor. So he then applied for a postponement of the hearing, but the judge refused to allow this as well. Forwood's next ploy was to apply for the hearing to be held before a special jury, but this too was refused by the increasingly exasperated judge, who ordered that a plea of not guilty be entered and the case proceed. Forwood, or Southey as perhaps we should now call him, refused to be defended by counsel but, on being told that he would have to take his defence wholly on himself, reluctantly agreed to be represented.

Southey's counsel's first gambit was to put forward a plea of insanity and he called a Dr Dulvey, who said he was of the opinion that Southey's mind was 'thoroughly unhinged. I noticed a wildness in his eyes and his pulse was very quick.' The doctor went on to say that Ernest Southey claimed that he had no faith or creed and that he rambled on about John Stuart Mill, the famous philosopher and social reformer, whose brilliant essay, *On Liberty*, had been published not long before.

The counsel for the prosecution interjected, to laughter from the public gallery, 'Well, that is no proof of insanity! You are aware that Mr Mill is the Member of Parliament for Westminster?'

When Stephen Forwood, alias Ernest Southey, was put in the witness box, he claimed to have killed under a sense of duty. He and Mrs White, the woman he frequently referred to as his wife, together with the children, had been wandering around London in a state of destitution and he thought it better that the children should be put out of their misery. He added that they had been refused admission to a refuge, which would have given them some respite, although he did not say why this was so. He appears to have said very little about the reasons why he killed his lawful wife, Emily, and their child, continually complaining about the poor hand life had dealt him and the extent of his own problems.

The defence of insanity having been rejected by the judge, the jury retired to consider their verdict but quickly returned to deliver a verdict of guilty. The sentence of death was duly passed.

In the condemned cell, Ernest Southey continued to rant about how unjust life was and wrote a long letter to the trial judge protesting about the illegality of the trial, having been prevented from conducting his own case. 'I am not insane. I should like to have my case argued before metaphysicians and philosophers for I believe my mind and motives would be a proper subject for psychological enquiry.'

Having blamed just about everybody else for the situation he now found himself in, Southey now turned his attention to Lord Dudley, claiming that his lordship's brother, the Honourable Dudley Ward, owed him around £1,200 from bets placed on games of billiards. The fact that Lord Dudley had refused to pay his brother's gambling debts prevented Southey from repaying money he had embezzled, or from providing his family (or families) with proper sustenance. Southey admitted that on several occasions he had planned the murder of one or other of the brothers.

It would seem that Forwood/Southey was seriously delusional and one cannot help wondering whether he would have been convicted of murder in modern times. However, the McNaghten Rules, formulated following the murder of Sir Robert Peel's secretary in 1843, required that it must be clearly proved that, at the time of committing the act, the accused was unaware of the nature of the act, or that what he was doing was wrong, and given Southey's statements before and after the trial, it seems unlikely that such a defence could succeed.

And so, on 11 January 1866, Stephen Forwood or Ernest Southey stepped onto the scaffold outside Maidstone Prison, where William Calcraft duly executed the sentence of the court, one of the last public executions to be held there.

Chapter 12

Drowned in the Dyke

The Romney Marsh can be an eerie place, where sea mists creep in from the English Channel across the flat, desolate landscape, criss-crossed by a labyrinth of drainage and irrigation dykes. The ancient towns of Romney, Lydd and Dungeness are sparsely inhabited even today, and the surrounding countryside can boast but a few scattered farmhouses and isolated cottages.

If this is true today, it was even more so in the nineteenth century. Apart from the desolation, the damp air was notoriously unhealthy – so much so that when a farmer complained about the loss of some sheep and the lack of police cover for his village in 1860, the Chief Constable of Kent responded that 'the constables stationed at Brookland have so suffered from fever and ague that their services at that station were for a long time scarcely nominal'.

Nevertheless, the soil is rich and fertile; sheep fed on the salt-sprayed grasslands produce fine lamb to accompany the potatoes which grow in the neighbouring fields.

The ancient Cinque Port of Hythe lies on the edge of the Marsh and it was here that, around this time, the Kidder family lived. William Kidder was a potato salesman and general dealer who often frequented the Romney Marsh to buy potatoes from the farmers there and do any other sort of business that came his way. It was on one of these business trips that he met and later married 25-year-old Frances, who moved to Hythe to live with her husband and William's 10-year-old illegitimate daughter from a previous affair, Louisa Kidder Staples.

That Frances resented this perpetual reminder of her husband's past life and misdeeds seems to have been well known in the area and there was a history of her violence towards her stepdaughter. Neighbours were later to testify that they had seen Frances throw

Louisa across the room, banging her head on the table and also that she had beaten the child so severely that she came downstairs screaming, her pinafore covered in blood. Sometimes the child was fed, sometimes not, depending on the mood of the stepmother.

When friends and neighbours remonstrated with Frances, she replied that she would do as she liked with the girl; if she wished she would poison her, she would murder her. Even Frances's sister was later to testify that Frances had often threatened to drown Louisa, but claimed that she said this without passion.

Another neighbour confirmed the history of beatings and said he had had to take Louisa in one cold night when she had been locked out of her house. No word was ever said against William Kidder and it is significant that the ill-treatment only occurred when he was absent.

During the summer of 1867, Frances went to spend some time with her parents, Francis Turner and his wife, in the town of New Romney, taking with her Louisa and her own 3-year-old child, Emma. The trio were welcomed by the older couple and were treated well by them.

Not long afterwards, on a fine Sunday evening in late August, the Turners left around seven o'clock to go for a walk, leaving Frances in the house with Louisa, Emma and two of the parents' own youngsters. When the parents returned about an hour later they were concerned to find their two children and Emma Kidder alone, with no sign of Frances or Louisa.

Knowing their daughter's mental state and her violent antipathy towards Louisa, it was not long before a search was mounted, which William Kidder joined as soon as he got the news. But before long Frances returned, alone, and when her mother asked her where Louisa was, she replied 'She's out there.' Concerned and suspicious, her mother asked, 'Have you made off with her?' to which Frances replied, 'No, no mother, I have not.' 'Where is she, then?' she was asked and, with a shrug, replied, 'I have no idea.' Upon which she went off to change her light-coloured, spotted muslin dress for a heavier, darker coloured one. She gave no reason for this unusual change of attire so late in the day.

Frances remained completely unresponsive to the questions put to her by various members of the family and so her husband and father went to fetch the local policeman, Constable Aspinall. Being acquainted with the facts, he interviewed the apparently unconcerned Frances and asked her, 'Do you know anything about this child?' to which she made no reply. Unable to get any sense out of Frances, the constable turned to William and said, 'What am I to do with your wife, Kidder?' The distressed father of the missing child responded, 'I shall give her in charge for wilful murder.'

The constable then took hold of Frances and took her to the local lock-up. On the way she told the officer that Louisa had fallen into a dyke and described the spot where this had occurred.

On his return the constable searched the house and found the light-coloured dress that Frances had been wearing earlier thrown into a corner of the bedroom, the hem wet and muddy.

Meanwhile the search for Louisa was continuing and, in the light of what Frances had told the policeman, concentrated on the series of dykes about a quarter of a mile from the home, and her poor little body was eventually found near the spot that Frances had described. The child had clearly drowned, which was something of a puzzle, since the water in the dyke was only a foot or so deep and a 10-year-old child could easily have clambered out – unless she was prevented from doing so. And if it was indeed an accident, as Frances was later to claim, why did she not run for help?

The circumstantial evidence was damning and Frances was charged with the murder of her stepdaughter and held in Maidstone Prison awaiting trial. As no Winter Assize was held that year, she had to wait until the Kent Spring Assize and it was not until March 1868 that she finally appeared in the dock, where she pleaded not guilty and insisted, 'I did not do it!'

In the witness box, she described how she and Louisa were making their way across the fields to meet her parents when two horses came running up to them. Louisa panicked and was so frightened by these beasts that she fell into the dyke which ran alongside the field. Frances said she jumped into the dyke to get her out. It was pointed out that the water in the dyke where the body was found was quite shallow and that a girl of Louisa's age would have had no difficulty in getting out by herself. The defence

The Romney Marsh dyke where Frances Kidder drowned her stepdaughter.

Another view of the deep dyke.

countered that Louisa had fallen in the dyke further along from where she was found and that her lifeless body had been washed down to the point where it eventually came to rest. The water where she fell in was much deeper and the banks steeper, which was why she could not get out and so drowned.

The prosecution then produced the light-coloured dress which Frances had been wearing and which the policeman had found in her bedroom. The prosecuting counsel made this piece of apparel a major factor in his cross-examination:

> *You say you jumped into the dyke to try to rescue Louisa but here is the dress you were wearing. Although when it was found it was muddied and the hem was damp, had you really jumped into deep water to rescue your stepdaughter, it would have been soaked through. I suggest the condition of the dress and the location where the child's body was found prove that it was indeed at this latter point that she met her death and that you held her under the shallow water with the wicked intention of doing away with her.*

The case against Frances Kidder was further strengthened by a stream of witnesses, who testified as to her character and behaviour. She was described as having 'manifested ungovernable fury' and was accused of having committed numerous acts of malicious damage which she then blamed on others.

The defence tried to show that there were mitigating circumstances. Frances was illiterate and came from a very poor background. Witnesses in her defence claimed that she had been badly trained by her parents and that her husband had subjected her to severe ill-treatment and abuse. It does seem that she was not particularly bright and possibly somewhat mentally deranged, but no plea of insanity under the McNaghten Rules was put forward by the defence.

But the desperate efforts made by Frances's defence were not enough to save her. The jury took only twelve minutes to return a verdict of guilty of wilful murder and there could be but one outcome of their decision. The judge, Mr Justice Byles, solemnly placed the square of black silk on his head and ordered that she be taken hence to a place of execution where she would be hanged by the neck until she be dead, 'And may the Lord have mercy on your soul.'

Taken to the condemned cell, Frances Kidder finally confessed her crime to the prison chaplain. While awaiting execution she frequently became hysterical and when the day finally came, on 2 April 1868, just three weeks after her trial, she had to be helped up the steps to the scaffold which had been erected outside Maidstone Prison. Once there, two warders held her in position on the trapdoors, where she prayed intently. The executioner, William Calcraft, made the final preparations, strapping her wrists in front of her and putting a leather strap around her body and arms at elbow level and another around her skirt to hold her long skirt down. A hood was placed over her head and the noose adjusted around her neck.

The trap was then released and Frances plunged down to her death. It was not a quick end and she struggled hard for two or three minutes before her life finally left her. As was so often the case where Calcraft was the executioner, her death was caused by strangulation rather than the breaking of her neck. Her body was left for the customary hour before being cut down, during which time the crowd of some 2,000 that had assembled to watch the event had dwindled away. The audience, many of them women and girls, would have been unaware that they had just witnessed the last public hanging of a woman in Britain.

Later the same month, Richard Bishop had the dubious distinction of being the last man to hang in public outside Maidstone Prison. He had stabbed a man in Sydenham who had complained about the noise Bishop was making.

In line with the Capital Punishment Within Prisons Act, passed by Parliament on 29 May 1868, all future hangings would take place within the prison walls, out of sight of the general public, so ending a spectacle which the people of Kent had enjoyed for a thousand years.

Chapter 13

Death of an Innocent

The murder of an innocent child is always viewed with horror by ordinary people and never more so than when the killer is the child's own mother. Since 1922 the defence of infanticide has been available to a mother who can show that, at the time of the crime, the balance of her mind was disturbed by reason of her not having fully recovered from the effect of giving birth. To be in a position to claim this defence under current legislation, the child must be under the age of twelve months (originally it was vaguely confined to the death of a 'newborn' infant), so, even had this comparatively modern law been in force in Victorian England, it would not have helped Anne Lawrence, who stood before the Kent Winter Assize in 1866, indicted for the murder of her 4-year-old son and the attempted murder of her lover.

The story begins in the early 1860s when 29-year-old Anne was living with her husband in Tunbridge Wells. The couple were friendly with a Walter Highams and this friendship developed into a torrid love affair between Highams and the good-looking Anne, which resulted in their leaving their respective spouses in 1864. Anne took her son, Benjamin, with her and the three of them set up home at 2 Ebury Cottages, Tunbridge Wells, where, shortly afterwards, Anne gave birth to another child, the father of whom was Walter Highams.

Perhaps because she was well aware that Highams had cheated on his wife and suspecting that he had a roving eye, Anne Lawrence was very jealous of her lover. By the time they had been together for two years, she had become convinced that he was having an affair with another woman. Things came to a head when Highams sent Anne to London to buy vegetables while he went off to Town Malling, where he appears to have spent the night. When Anne

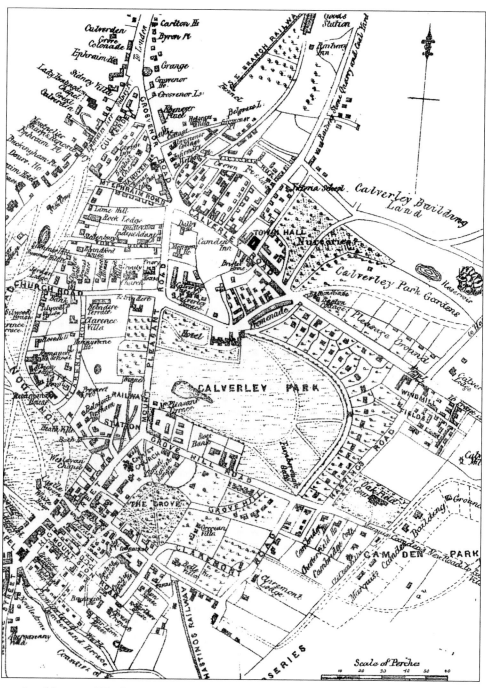

An old map of Tunbridge Wells, showing the town as it existed in the early nineteenth century. Although Ebury Cottages are not shown (and have since been demolished) the map does show the early town hall and police station. Tunbridge Wells Library.

found out on her return she was furious and a violent row developed.

The pair nevertheless went to bed together that night, with young Benjamin sleeping at the foot of the bed and the newborn baby in the bed with them.

Some time between four and five o'clock in the morning Highams awoke to find Anne standing over him, chopping at his head with a bill hook. Covered in blood, he tried desperately to defend himself but she continued to hack at him frenziedly until she was exhausted. Only then did she cease her assault and leave him to go downstairs.

Highams staggered out of bed, bleeding profusely from his multiple wounds, and followed her downstairs, where Anne renewed her violent attack. By this time, however, alerted by the noise, a number of neighbours had arrived and came to his rescue. They restrained the hysterical and abusive Anne with some difficulty and sent a message to the Tunbridge Wells police station. Chief Superintendent John Embury, the man in charge of the borough's police force, attended the scene very promptly, assisted by other officers.

As if the sight of the bloodied Highams was not disturbing enough, an even more horrifying scene awaited the policemen when they mounted the stairs to the bedroom. Lying at the foot of the bed they found young Benjamin, his throat cut so violently that his little head was nearly severed from his body. The razor which had been used to cause the fatal injury was found discarded in the room.

'It was Walter,' quickly claimed Anne when questioned by the police. 'I would never harm my child. That is why I attacked him.'

Although the officers found some blood on Anne's clothing, this could have come from her paramour's wounds. There did not seem to be as much as one might have expected from a severed jugular vein or carotid artery. It is true that the razor belonged to Highams and it is also true that he claimed not to have noticed Benjamin's body on the bed when he got up, but there is no doubt that Highams was suffering badly from his wounds, with blood all over his face, and had no reason to examine the boy. And Anne had easy access to his razor.

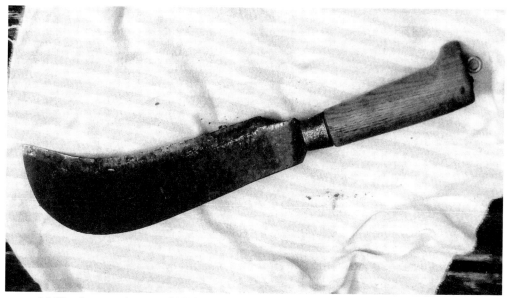

A billhook, as used to attack Walter Highams.

So who did the deed? The evidence was inconclusive and there appeared to be no real motive. Was it the mother, Anne Lawrence, or her live-in lover, Walter Highams? The difficult decision was finally taken and Chief Superintendent Embury charged Anne with the murder of Benjamin Lawrence and the felonious wounding of Walter Highams. She appeared at the West Kent Assizes in Maidstone in December 1866, where she pleaded not guilty. 'I declare before God and man that I did not kill the child ... I am innocent!' she declared vehemently. But, having heard the evidence, such as it was, the jury took only three hours to return a verdict of guilty. There could only be one sentence and Anne Lawrence was condemned to be hanged by the neck until she was dead.

Despite her protestations, Anne Lawrence later admitted that it was she who had killed her son, saying that she cut his throat while he lay in bed. As for the lack of blood on her clothing, she said she had purposely held her body back to avoid this happening, perhaps more out of vanity or fastidiousness, rather than a deliberate attempt to cover her tracks. She then decided to blame Walter Highams to punish him for his infidelities.

Anne Lawrence's motive for killing her son was never really called into question, nor satisfactorily explained. Was it deliberately done with the whole idea of getting Highams arrested and punished for his waywardness, or was there some other reason for the murder, and the shifting of the blame onto her lover merely done to cover up her actions? We shall never know.

Like many of her class in mid-Victorian times, Anne Lawrence was poorly educated but she was described as possessing 'considerable natural acquirements' and her intellect was 'very superior to the ordinary class of persons'. She was also vain and proud of her looks, even in the face of imminent death, and enquired whether she would be hanged in her ordinary clothes and if she would be allowed to wear her bonnet for her last appearance in public.

Anne may have felt that her last moments before the large crowd outside Maidstone Prison were somewhat overshadowed by the fact that there was to be a double hanging. The authorities had decided that both she and 20-year-old James Fletcher, condemned to death at the same assizes for the killing of a warder at Chatham prison, should be hanged together. This would mean the scaffold only had to be erected once, and there would be just one cost for the soldiers to guard it and only one train fare for William Calcraft, the executioner, who might also be persuaded to carry out the hangings on a sort of 'two for the price of one' arrangement. The magistrates who ran the county were notoriously keen to save money in any way possible.

And so, shortly after noon on 10 January 1867, the two unconnected prisoners were both 'launched into eternity' before a much larger crowd than usual, containing many 'apparently decent' women and girls. Despite the obvious antipathy towards this mother who had cold-bloodedly murdered her own little son, the crowd was reported as being well-behaved.

Chapter 14

Death at Dover Priory

Thomas Wells was an 18-year-old carriage cleaner and porter at Dover Priory railway station in the heyday of rail travel in the middle of the nineteenth century. Poorly educated, from an impecunious but honest family, Thomas was a typical teenager before that term was ever invented. He was continually at odds with the world around him, resentful of criticism, disrespectful of authority and generally felt the world owed him a living – a state of mind no working-class person could entertain in the nineteenth century.

At his work he had a history of lateness and insubordination and the stationmaster at Dover Priory station, 60-year-old Adolphus Walshe, had had to rebuke and report him on several occasions. Towards the end of April 1868, the stationmaster told Wells to take a barrowload of manure down to the superintendent's flower garden at the Harbour railway station, but Wells flatly refused. 'That's not my job,' he surlily responded.

Despite repeated instructions to carry out his orders, Wells persisted in his refusal and made some sarcastic and offensive remark to the stationmaster, prompting the latter to write a report to Henry Cox, the superintendent in charge of Dover's two railway stations, complaining yet again about Wells's behaviour. As a result, the superintendent went to Dover Priory station on 1 May 1868, where he interviewed Wells in the presence of Mr Walshe. He was later to describe Wells as having 'a very vindictive look and he made some pert remark to Walshe'. Such was Wells's temper that he was sent away for ten minutes to cool down.

On his return, Mr Cox asked Wells if he was prepared to apologize to Mr Walshe, but Wells made no reply. The interview, such as it was, lasted another ten minutes or so, after which Wells left. Cox and Walshe remained in the office for a while, discussing

The stationmaster's office, now referred to as the Station Supervisor's office, where the murder took place.

what they were going to do about this recalcitrant young man. Suddenly, there was the sound of a gunshot and Walshe fell to the ground, mortally wounded. Looking up, Cox saw Wells standing about two yards outside the office, holding a rifle. Calling for help, Cox did what he could for his colleague but there was no hope. The grievously injured man was too far gone and died shortly afterwards. By this time a messenger had been sent to the Dover police station house, which was then in Queen Street, to report the incident and call for urgent assistance.

Sergeant George Stevens of the Dover Borough Police attended the scene with all the majesty of the law. He found Wells, sitting in one of the carriages, leaning on a cushion, with a gun in his left hand. 'You must deliver up the gun to me,' he intoned, conscious of his position as the representative of the law. He was perhaps a little surprised and not a little relieved when Wells obliged without demur. 'You must come out of the carriage,' was the next order and, once again, Wells did as he was told.

By this time, Superintendent John Coram, the man in charge of the Dover police force, had arrived and took over. He examined the weapon and found an exploded cap on the nipple of the gun and discovered another two in Wells's pocket. The murder weapon was delivered to a local gunsmith, William Newton, who concluded that it had been fired within the last two hours, thus confirming that it was indeed the gun used to shoot down Adolphus Walshe.

A clear case of wilful and premeditated murder, it would seem, and Wells was duly charged. A brief appearance before the Dover magistrates and Wells was remanded to the next Kent Assizes at Maidstone.

The case for the prosecution seemed clear-cut. A surgeon who had examined the body of the deceased stated that there was a large wound to the face, destroying the nose, fracturing the upper jaw and with an exit wound at the back of the head. The actual bullet was found on the mantelpiece in the office, having passed completely through the victim's head.

The defence put forward by Wells's counsel was that the defendant was not responsible for his actions, as he was suffering from the effects of an accident which had occurred at the railway station nearly a year ago. When questioned by the counsel for the defence, Mr Cox stated that he was unaware of any such incident and that Wells had not taken any time off sick at that time. Wells's mother, however, was quite adamant: the previous August, she claimed, her son had been brought home 'much injured' and bleeding from the nose and mouth. She had been told that he had been caught between the buffers of a train while coupling or uncoupling carriages. The family apparently did not call a doctor, even though Wells belonged to a benefit club, but a motherly neighbour 'did what was necessary'. The young man remained in bed for a week.

It was after this accident that Thomas Wells was said to have begun acting strangely. One night he came downstairs and tried to drag his mother out of bed. He would move tables and chairs around for no real reason – simply a compulsive action. In the end they had to fasten the windows and lock the doors to prevent him from getting out. Since the alleged accident, his demeanour had changed markedly. Sometimes he got very excited over trivial matters or for no reason at all and his bulging eyes seemed ready to bolt out of his head. At other times he simply acted very childishly.

Thomas's father corroborated this story and told the court that he was the owner of the rifle concerned. He went on to say that, about a week before the murder, he lent this gun to his son, who wanted it to keep birds off the garden he tended by the railway station. Thomas said he used to hide the gun in one of the carriages, as he was afraid it would get stolen if he left it in the porters' room. Other witnesses said that Thomas, together with one or two other young lads, had played about with the gun, as if it were a toy, seemingly unconscious or reckless of its deadly capabilities.

The fact that only the parents appeared to have remarked upon the change in Thomas's behaviour after the accident – if indeed there had been an accident, since no doctor had been in attendance and the railway superintendent was unaware of it, though he surely should have known of it – obviously influenced the jury's brief discussions, as did the history of insubordination and 'pertness' and they returned a verdict of guilty of wilful murder after but a brief retirement. There could only be one outcome.

The Wig and Gown *public house, formerly the* New Inn, *where the executioner used to take refreshment before his grisly task. The inn was demolished around the 1960s.* Photo © copyright Kent Messenger Group.

On 13 August 1868, a horse-drawn cab drew up outside the *New Inn* (later known as the *Wig and Gown* and now demolished to make way for yet more office accommodation), which stood quite close to Maidstone Prison, and a corpulent, elderly man, white-haired and with a white beard, alighted and went inside. The arrival was William Calcraft, the public executioner, who soon emerged from the inn and walked towards the prison gate. He did not choose to walk the shortest route – there were iron railings around the courthouse yard and he followed the course of these, even though it made his journey longer. His face was half turned towards the railings as if eager to avoid the attention of a ragged troupe of men and boys who were running to meet him. Dressed in a suit of black broadcloth, with black leather gloves and a chimney-pot hat, carrying a shabby carpet bag, a gold chain and pendant across his ample stomach, he might have been a comfortable member of the middle class. That is, according to contemporary reports:

William Calcraft, the executioner.

> *until you saw his face. It would be fanciful to say his dreadful calling was written on it, yet there is something in its half-frowning, half-callous look which suggests evil and the boys who rushed up to look closely at the man who was about to hang Wells, turned away laughing when he disappeared behind the prison door.*

The boys proudly aired their knowledge of what the carpet bag might contain: straps and buckles to pinion the arms and legs of the condemned man and, most importantly, the rope with its noose. No doubt their youthful imaginations conjured up other paraphernalia which they thought a hangman might carry in his bag.

Since this was to be one of the first executions which would not be carried out in public, the waiting crowd was smaller than usual and the executioner's arrival was the only feeble spasm of excitement which it enjoyed.

On this occasion Calcraft was assisted by one Smith of Dudley, a very different man from the experienced and rather pompous executioner. As the *Kentish Express* reported:

> *None of the varnish of respectability here. A capacious velveteen jacket and waistcoat, a broad-striped shirt and one of those closely-shaven, close cropped faces with restless ferrety eyes to be seen in abundance whenever the London rough is to the fore, made this man recall the prize ring, the betting list.*

Inside the prison, Thomas Wells was wearing his London, Chatham and Dover Railway Company uniform corduroy suit, joining the chaplain in a hymn. Even when the white cotton nightcap was pulled over his head by Calcraft he continued to sing. He was still singing as Calcraft nodded to Smith and, with a hideous clatter, the false floor gave way and the song was cut short as the singer swung silently in the air. The tiny audience of officials and representatives of the press saw a few convulsive struggles of Wells's legs, a gurgling in the throat and a rapid clenching of the hands which were rapidly turning blue and then all was still. Thomas Wells had paid the ultimate price for his teenage tantrums.

Chapter 15

A Kentish Luddite

Rural Kent in the 1870s was a seething hotbed of discontent. More and more machinery was being introduced to replace or reduce reliance on human labour; the winter of 1878–9 had been a particularly hard one, with severe frosts rendering the earth unworkable. There was little work for the agricultural labourers to do and many were laid off by their farmer employers, unwilling to pay the men to stand around and do nothing. Those who retained their jobs did so only if they were willing to agree to a harsh cut in wages to as low as half-a-crown a day. In Wingham, between Canterbury and Sandwich, more than seventy men were locked out for refusing to accept such a swingeing cut in their meagre earnings. Large numbers began looking to start a new life in New Zealand or Australia.

The steam engine used by the Gillow family for threshing and ploughing purposes, the subject of acts of sabotage. Sandwich Guildhall Archive.

It is in the shadow of this turbulent situation that our story begins. Captain William Gillow JP was an important landowner, who farmed several holdings in and around Woodnesborough, near Sandwich in East Kent. He was a go-ahead farmer and was keen to make use of all the new labour-saving devices which were coming on the market. Recently he had acquired a steam ploughing machine which was being used on his Marshborough farmholding. This innovation was not universally welcomed, however, and during November 1878, there had been incidents in which damage was caused to the steam engine by the deliberate smashing of the steam and water gauges, rendering the machine unusable until repairs could be carried out. The local members of the county constabulary were informed but, not surprisingly, they had little success in tracing the culprit, despite the fact that this sort of offence was a felony under the Malicious Damage Act of 1861, punishable by a long sentence of penal servitude.

Arthur Gillow was Captain Gillow's son and managed Marshborough farm for his father. He was generally well liked by his workers, who were nevertheless respectful of this scion of such an important family and who held their livelihoods in his hands. Arthur was a strong, healthy man and was very active. In addition to being very much a hands-on farm manager, he was a keen runner and a member of the Woodnesborough Running Club.

The last time Arthur Gillow was seen alive was around 11.15 pm on 4 December 1878. He had had a few drinks in the local pub but was sober and perfectly fit and well. He told a witness to whom he had been chatting that he had to leave as he 'had a job on'. He did not explain further but strode off into the darkness, swinging his stick as he went. Subsequent events suggest this 'job' was a visit to the ploughing engine to check that it had not been vandalized once more.

A little before five o'clock the following December morning, a farm labourer by the name of William Drayson set off from his home in order to start work. It was still completely dark, as the sky was overcast, obscuring any light from the moon or the stars to relieve the blackness. At that time of the year the sun would not rise for some hours and there were no such things as street lights in the

Photo of Arthur Gillow, taken by a local photographer, shortly before his death.
Sandwich Guildhall Archive.

Kentish countryside. William Drayson's route took him past the field where the newly repaired steam engine lay, although of course it was too dark to see it. At one point he thought he heard a rustling but saw no one and put the noise down to fox or a badger foraging for food.

However, about 10 yards past the engine, he suddenly all but tripped over a recumbent figure, lying with its feet in the road and the head and shoulders on the grass verge. Assuming it to be a drunk who had passed out or was sleeping off a particularly heavy night in the open, despite the freezing weather, Drayson kicked the feet of the still figure in an attempt to awaken him and also to work off some of the displeasure he felt at being nearly tripped up. He could not see whose body it was but he took hold of its hands and attempted to pull the 'drunk' to his feet. To his horror, the hands were wet, stiff and freezing cold and Drayson realized he was dealing with a dead body.

Alarmed at his discovery and still unaware of the identity of the dead man, Drayson retraced his steps to the village to seek help. He went to the house of his uncle, whom he awoke and, now armed with a lantern, the couple made their way to the scene of the incident. By the dim light of the lantern they could see that the head and shoulders of the body were lying in a pool of blood; this was no drunk who had frozen to death but the victim of a violent and mortal assault. Even with the limited illumination provided by the lantern, it was still not possible to identify the body because of the blood which had congealed on the features.

With no means of lifting the body, and deciding that it was perhaps best left where it lay, the two men returned to Woodnesborough where they reported to the local constable before going on to seek the advice of their employer, Captain Gillow, in his capacity as a justice of the peace. On the gallant captain's instructions, the two men then returned to the scene with a better lantern to await the arrival of Constable Stone.

By the light of this more powerful means of illumination, the two men could see that there were two walking sticks lying near the body, one of which was broken in half. When the constable arrived they pointed out these sticks to him and the three men then managed to lift the body and carry it to the coach house at the farm. Here the body was finally identified as Arthur Gillow by means of the ring worn on one finger, the features being still unrecognizable.

Arthur's brother, Richard, was informed of the death around 6.15 that morning and promptly went to his father's house, where he saw the battered body of his brother lying in the coach house. Determined to get justice for his brother's violent demise, Richard went to Sandwich Police Station where he demanded that they telegraph for a detective. Once he was satisfied that the wheels of the law had been set in motion, he made his way to the scene of the murder, where he examined the steam engine. He was not too surprised to find that the two gauges had again been smashed and, since they had been perfectly all right the day before, the damage had obviously been done during the night. He also saw a pool of dried blood on the Sandwich road some ten yards away from the engine, around which there were a lot of footmarks. When Sergeant Corder arrived on the scene, Richard Gillow assisted him in taking plaster casts of the more pronounced of these prints and, later that day, when Superintendent Ovenden arrived from the Bearsted Division to assist with the investigation, he accompanied the superintendent when he went to compare these casts with the boots worn by one of the Gillows' workers, Stephen Gambrill.

Stephen Gambrill was rapidly becoming the prime suspect for the murder of Arthur Gillow. Gambrill was a 28-year-old man, a little over medium height and, although sparely built, he was widely recognized as a powerful and athletic man, a member of the same running club as the dead man. He was employed as a waggoner on Marshborough Farm and lived in a cottage on the farm.

The man in charge of the Wingham Division of the Kent County Constabulary was Superintendent Stokes, who had held that post ever since the constabulary was formed in 1857. (He was to retire the following month after twenty-two years' service in the rank.) His divisional headquarters was at Sandwich Police Station and, like most senior police officers in those days, he lived 'over the shop' in accommodation provided at the station. As a long-serving and senior police officer and as the murder had taken place within his division, Superintendent Stokes was in charge of the

investigation, assisted by his colleagues Superintendent Ovenden
from Bearsted and Superintendent Walker from the Home
(Canterbury) Division and a detective who had been sent from
New Scotland Yard. The allocation of three superintendents to such
a case was extremely unusual and is indicative of the importance
with which the Gillow family was regarded by the chief constable.

Gambrill was interviewed at the scene by Superintendent Stokes,
who became suspicious of his replies. His clothing was bloodstained
and very dirty and his boots matched the plaster casts taken at the
scene. Constable Stone, the village policeman, reported that he had
seen Gambrill in the village just before midnight and so he was
definitely up and about when the crime was committed.

Following further enquiries around the district, Gambrill was
brought to Sandwich Police Station by Superintendent Walker and
a constable around four o'clock that afternoon. He was not under
arrest and was merely 'helping the police with their enquiries' – an
important distinction, as future events were to show.

Gambrill was not placed in a cell but was seated on a form by the
charge-room table in the police station. Having complained of
feeling cold, he had been provided with a blanket which he wrapped
around himself. Around 8.30 that evening, the station officer,
Constable Reader, noticed that Gambrill had wrapped the blanket
around his head and was now lying down on the form and then saw
blood dripping from the form to the floor. He rushed over, removed
the blanket and saw that Gambrill's throat had been cut. As he did
so, a knife dropped from the suspect's hand. Medical assistance was
sought but the wound proved to be superficial and did not require
hospital treatment.

At the subsequent trial, questions would be raised as to why he
had not been searched and the knife found and confiscated, but the
police insisted that he was not a prisoner at that stage and therefore
they were not entitled to search him.

Later that same evening, Superintendents Stokes and Walker,
together with the Metropolitan Police detective, returned from
Woodnesborough, where they had been carrying out further
enquiries, and formally charged Gambrill with the murder of
Arthur Gillow. He was kept in the police station until the following

Monday morning, when he was remanded in custody and conveyed to St Augustine's Gaol in Canterbury.

In the gaol Gambrill shared a cell with another prisoner, Edward Broad, who later was to tell the trial jury that he was present when Gambrill was visited by his brother and sister-in-law. After they had gone, Gambrill confided to Broad, 'I'm all right now.' 'How's that?' Broad responded.

That man that I knocked down and kicked is dead. I'm sure I shall be hung. I shall go and see old Marwood [the hangman]. I shouldn't care if it wasn't for my wife and two children but they will be all right. I've plenty of good friends and thirteen score of pork in the tub and plenty of potatoes, a ton of coal, a good parsnip bed and a good house of things. She can either keep them or sell them.

Another prisoner told the court that he heard Gambrill say,

That man is dead that I knocked down. I knocked him down and used my foot on him and after I done it I went home and I eat a good supper and had a good night's sleep. I've had my revenge if I get hung.

Gambrill also told one of the warders that the killing was done in self-defence, but it was later shown that there were no marks of violence on his body.

Stephen Gambrill appeared before the Kent Assizes in Maidstone in January 1879. The proceedings were delayed for some time by the defence counsel's objection to a number of the empanelled jurors, who were from the county area, presumably on the grounds that they were of the farming or landowning class and so biased against the prisoner. In the end a new jury was formed consisting almost entirely of residents of Maidstone.

Apart from the evidence of the two prisoners mentioned above, the court heard from a surgeon that the injuries suffered by the victim could have been caused by sticks but the majority were inflicted by boots. A further examination had revealed that the victim's throat had also been cut, probably with the same knife as that used by the prisoner in his abortive suicide attempt in the police station. A cobbler identified the boots which matched the plaster casts as having been made by him for Gambrill.

The defence made great play of the fact that the accused and the victim were on good terms. The workers on Marshborough Farm were not on strike and there was no significant dispute over wages. Was it not possible that Gambrill, as a loyal and hard-working employee, went to check the engine that evening to ensure that it had not been damaged? Perhaps he went there to hoping to catch the saboteur and thus be able to claim the £10 reward. Perhaps Gillow and Gambrill met and both thought, in the dark, that the other was the person who was damaging the machine.

One might think that these questions should properly have been put to the accused in the witness box, but the procedures at that time prevented any such action: the prisoner was not entitled to give evidence in his own defence, nor could his counsel relate to the court anything the prisoner told him. Everything rested on the various witnesses and the skill and plausibility of the opposing barristers.

At the conclusion of the hearing, for reasons best known to himself, the judge tore the defence case to shreds in his summing up and it was therefore no surprise that the jury returned after just a fifteen-minute retirement to find Gambrill guilty of the wilful murder of his employer, Arthur Gillow.

In the event, the prison chaplain later told the press that, on the morning of his execution, Gambrill had told him that he was caught in the act of breaking the gauges on the steam engine. There was a struggle and Arthur Gillow was felled by a blow from Gambrill's walking stick, which broke in half with the force of the impact. Fearful that his victim might recover and accuse him, Gambrill 'finished the job' by cutting the unconscious man's throat.

And so Gambrill's premonition came to pass and, on 4 February 1879, he was hanged inside Maidstone Prison by William Marwood, who had now replaced William Calcraft as the principal public executioner.

Chapter 16

Death in the Pleasure Grounds

The town of Gravesend has stood contentedly beside the Thames Estuary for more than a millennium. It was there in the eleventh century, when the Domesday Book recorded it as 'Gravesham' – a title which the district has re-adopted in recent years. It became an incorporated borough under Queen Elizabeth I.

Going back just over a century, the town was a comparatively wealthy borough of some 23,000 souls with a thriving boat-building, fishing, ferry and piloting business and was proudly referred to as the boundary port for London. Until the arrival of the railways it had seen many crowned heads of Europe and other important dignitaries land there on their way to London to be received by the monarch.

In the late nineteenth century, the worthy burgers of Gravesend would often spend their evenings and weekends enjoying the facilities offered within the Subscription Pleasure Grounds on the Wrotham Road and perhaps see a play or a show in the Pavilion Theatre there.

These well-used facilities were owned and operated by one Thomas Eves, who in 1882 was aged around fifty-three. One of a large family, he was a native of Gravesend, the son of a local builder, and his present position in Gravesend society was entirely due to his hard work and business acumen.

Thomas Eves was a married man with five children and had previously owned a small nursery in the Woodlands Park area, where he grew good-quality vegetables, which were much sought after by the locals. However, when he was around forty years of age, he left his wife and family and set up home with, and later married, Annie, the widow of England Clarke. One might suspect that this was a marriage of convenience since the late Mr Clarke

The bandstand in the Subscription Pleasure Grounds. Photo courtesy of Gravesend Library.

owned the Wrotham Road Nurseries, between the *Bat and Ball* public house and Old Road West and was a rival to Thomas Eves. The marriage to Annie Clarke meant that Eves now controlled the two main nurseries in the area, which, over the course of the next few years, he transformed into the Subscription Grounds, a pleasure garden to which the public was admitted on payment of sixpence entry fee. There was a bandstand, and open-air concerts were held here in the summer, the best available bands and concert talent being engaged.

In 1879, to enable him to extend his concert season, Thomas Eves built a small theatre in the Pleasure Grounds, which he named the Pavilion. The building was sited in the Wrotham Road, the entrance to the theatre being exactly where Essex Road now lies. Built of timber and clad with corrugated iron, this edifice was quite a simple affair externally, but the interior was most artistically

The Pavilion Theatre in the Pleasure Grounds in 1884. From an original drawing by Tom Green.

Interior of the Pavilion Theatre about 1882. From an original drawing by Tom Green.

decorated with busts of Shakespeare, Milton, Byron, and others adorning one wall. Very soon concerts and theatrical performances were being offered to the public throughout the year.

In 1882 a young man by the name of William Clarke arrived in Gravesend from Canada. The 16-year-old was anxious to find employment and readily agreed to work for Thomas Eves as his ostler and general labourer for the lowly wage of five shillings. Clarke was also given room and board in the Eves's home, Manor Farmhouse in Pelham Road.

Thomas Eves was not an easy man to work for and was a demanding employer, but young Clarke was not easily cowed and was quick to come back with a saucy answer to Eves's sharply delivered orders and criticisms.

On Saturday 18 November 1882 Thomas Eves paid his staff their weekly wages but, when it came to Clarke's turn, he was sixpence short and could only give the lad four shillings and sixpence. Clarke was not best pleased, as there seemed to be no guarantee that he would eventually get the sixpence he was owed, and which was a sizeable slice out of his meagre pocket money.

It was Thomas Eves's practice to visit the Pleasure Grounds on a Sunday to catch up with his paperwork and write up the accounts and, as was customary, William Clarke took his boss his lunch in the office the day after the wages problem. Having completed his errand, Clarke went back to his lodgings in Manor Farmhouse and then returned to the Subscription Grounds with Mrs Eves's housemaid, Elizabeth Gwalter, for a walk round the gardens. Clarke went in through the gate and walked down to the office and called out, 'All right, sir?' Mr Eves responded, 'Have you watered the pony?' Clarke replied in the affirmative and was dismissed by Mr Eves. Clarke emerged to join Elizabeth by the gate nearest to the *Bat and Ball* public house and confided that he had noticed two young women sitting by the office fire, chatting to Thomas Eves.

The couple then decided to walk down the cricket field and round the Subscription Grounds. During their perambulations, William Clarke made a number of critical comments to his companion about Mr Eves associating with young women and neglecting his wife. 'If it was my mother I dare say she would kill him,' Elizabeth agreed. 'I dare say my mother would limb him.'

'Do you know what I am going to do, Lizzie?' Clarke continued. 'I mean to pop the governor off.'

Elizabeth could hardly believe what she was hearing. 'What are you talking about this afternoon, Fred?' she asked.

'I mean it,' replied Clarke (for some reason known to Elizabeth as 'Fred'), and when he was asked why, he elaborated, 'For being up here on a Sunday, and if I could get a six barrelled revolver I mean to do for the governor.'

The young girl was becoming more and more concerned about Clarke's threats: 'You are talking very serious this afternoon, Fred. I don't know what you mean.'

'If I could get a blank cartridge I would shoot the governor somewhere about the ribs, not to kill him, but to make him suffer,' responded the youth.

Elizabeth had had enough by now and started to leave, followed by Clarke, who locked the gate behind him. They walked back to Manor Farmhouse, where Elizabeth later told Mrs Eves of her conversation with Clarke that afternoon.

William Clarke had already told Mrs Eves on a number of occasions that her husband was entertaining ladies in his office, but she had taken no notice and there seems to have been no real substance in Clarke's allegations. Mrs Eves dismissed the tales as mere tittle-tattle, but she might have been more concerned about this latest revelation had she known that, a couple of weeks earlier, Clarke and his friend, Charlie Henderson, had been trying to find someone to sell them a revolver.

As it happened, the two young ladies in the office with Mr Eves on that fateful Sunday were members of the family of a theatrical 'digs' landlady who regularly accommodated the performers at the Pavilion. Thomas Eves had simply invited them into his office to shelter from the rain and to get out of the cold.

At six o'clock Clarke was sent back to the Subscription Grounds with his master's tea and was told by him to return around 9.30 with the pony and trap to take him home. Around 9.40, William Clarke called at the farmhou. .d asked Mrs Eves if she had seen her husband, saying that he had gone to collect him as ordered but had been unable to make him hear. Mrs Eves was not too perturbed at this stage and she instructed Clarke to return to the

Subscription Grounds and try again. Clarke went off and returned about half an hour later, saying he was still unable to raise Mr Eves.

It was now after ten o'clock on a dark, cold and wet winter's evening and Mrs Eves was by now getting really alarmed. She therefore sent William Clarke to fetch John Eves, Thomas's son by his former marriage, who was a fishmonger in Parrock Street. Clarke and John Eves set off together for the Subscription Grounds and, on their way, they bumped into Constable Easton of the Gravesend Borough Police in Wrotham Road and sought his aid. Clarke was in a very excitable state and said to the constable, 'My master is missing; will you come with me to try and find him? Something has happened to him I'm sure.' When asked how he knew this, Clarke replied, 'I have been up there at half-past nine, the time he ordered me, and shouted as usual and got no answer.'

The trio arrived at the darkened gardens and entered through the unlocked gate near the conservatory. Clarke immediately began to call out, 'Master! Master! Master!' until Constable Easton told him to keep cool. By the dim light of the constable's bull's-eye lantern they first searched the conservatory near the entrance gate before moving on to the office. The door was locked so the constable kicked it, following which a sound was heard from an outhouse by the office. Making his way there, the constable saw Mr Eves, standing with his head resting against the wall. He was covered in blood from a severe head wound, his face bruised and disfigured, the eyes barely visible through the swelling. His suit was torn and covered in blood.

Constable Easton hurried up to him and said, 'It's all right now, Mr Eves, I am a policeman.' Eves slowly raised his head and, seeing the reassuring uniform, grasped the constable's tunic and fell against him. He was unable to speak but managed to convey to the constable that he had been tripped up and robbed of his watch. Not realizing just how badly Thomas Eves had been injured, the party helped him to walk as far as the road where, seeing that more help was needed, the constable dispatched John Eves to the police station to get a stretcher, Clarke having disappeared by this time. Leaving Mr Eves leaning on the gate, the constable went across to a house in Portland Road opposite to get a brandy for the injured man. Meanwhile, William Clarke had hurried back to Manor Farmhouse in a very excited state, to break the news to Mrs Eves.

Police Constable Osborne arrived in response to John Eves's news and the two officers carried Mr Eves to the Infirmary, where a massive fracture of the skull was diagnosed. This appeared to have been caused by several blows to the head with a heavy, blunt instrument. By this time the victim had passed out and in fact never regained consciousness.

It seems that, earlier that evening, Thomas Eves left his office, locking the door behind him, and was attacked as he walked along the path leading to the gate. There is no doubt that he had put up a struggle, as there were several overturned flower pots, crushed bushes and trampled flowers at the scene. His billy-cock hat was found trodden into the mud and his false teeth had fallen out and been smashed. Barely conscious, Thomas Eves lay for some time in a pool of his own blood before he managed to struggle to his feet and grope his way to the outhouse where he was eventually discovered by the constable.

The next morning, Elizabeth Gwalter arrived at the Manor Farmhouse to start work and was surprised to find her mistress already up (in fact she had not been to bed) and in tears. On being told what had occurred, she turned to Clarke and said, 'Oh, Fred, you've shot him!' Clarke simply laughed and answered, 'No, I have not. I don't have a pistol.' Mrs Eves said she was sure it could not have been Clarke.

Fortunately, not everyone was so trusting. Superintendent George Berry was the head of the Gravesend Borough Police and a man of considerable police experience. He naturally took charge of the investigation and noticed that, among the maze of footprints around the scene of the attack, there was one set which appeared to match the hob-nailed boots worn by Clarke. He examined the clothes which the lad had been wearing the previous day and found them to be extremely muddy and spattered with blood. Clarke claimed to have been involved in a fight a fortnight previously, but Mrs Eves said that his clothes had been clean when he left the house around 6.30 the evening before, when he had taken Mr Eves's tea to him. Elizabeth Gwalter confirmed this: 'He was wearing those boots on Sunday. He said he had given eight shillings and sixpence for them. He put a clean shirt on last Sunday and wore it all the week.'

Although the watch was not found in his possession, when Elizabeth Gwalter told the superintendent what Clarke had said the previous evening, he was convinced that he had found the culprit and Clarke was arrested on a charge of causing grievous bodily harm under the Offences Against the Person Act of 1861.

Early the next morning, Thomas Eves died, never having regained consciousness. A message was sent to Mr Knowles, the carpenter who did all the carpentry jobs at the Pleasure Grounds and had built the Pavilion, to construct a suitable coffin for his old friend. Charlie Henderson, William Clarke's pal who worked for Mr Knowles, became very agitated when he heard the news of Mr Eves's death and later in the day he was found to have absconded.

In fact, Charlie had made his way to the West India Docks in London, where he tried to find a ship to take him abroad, but without success. He quickly struck up a friendship with a shop boy by the name of James Bartlett and was invited to stay at the latter's lodgings in return for half the rent. Over the next few days the two boys spent a lot of time together, visiting the coffee shops and going to the theatre. During this time, Charles Henderson spoke a great deal about the Gravesend murder and murder in general – so much so that James's suspicions were aroused and he finally went to the police to voice his concerns. On the Sunday following that of the murder, the two boys were walking along Bishopsgate Street when a police detective stopped them and, after a few questions, arrested Charles on suspicion of having committed the murder of Thomas Eves in Gravesend. When Charles was searched, pieces of a watch were found, together with a watch chain and locket, which Mrs Eves later identified as belonging to her late husband. A piece of silver which Charlie Henderson had sold to a jeweller in Houndsditch for one shilling and fourpence was recovered and identified by a local watchmaker as having come from Mr Eves's watch.

Henderson was taken back to Gravesend, where he was charged with the murder. He replied, 'I and Clarke done it with a long stick.' He refused to say any more, but this was enough.

Thomas Eves was buried the next day, Monday, and the adjourned inquest reopened the following day. The two prisoners, Clarke and Henderson, were driven up the hill from the police station at the town hall to the new County Court building in King Street, through a large crowd of sightseers, all anxious to catch a glimpse of the perpetrators of this vicious crime.

With the dock full of journalists, Clarke and Henderson were seated in front of the bench where the Coroner was presiding over the proceedings. Clarke, the lad who was ever ready with a saucy response to his late employer, evidently regarded himself as the star attraction. According to one of the journalists present,

He looked round and nodded and smiled to some acquaintances in the crowd; he chatted familiarly with the officer who had charge of him.

The fact of being alone in England, with no one to support him or pay for his defence, did not seem to concern Clarke unduly, even though his friend Henderson was represented by a solicitor paid for by his far from wealthy parents. After a long procession of witnesses, including Mrs Eves, her maid Elizabeth, and several policemen, during which Henderson appeared to fall asleep, the inquest was adjourned for two days. When it was resumed, Clarke took the stand and made a long statement to the effect that he had been struck with a stick by some boys, which accounted for the bruise on his head and the blood on his clothes. However, previous medical evidence had shown that the small bruise or contusion above Clarke's left ear would not have been such as to produce the amount of blood which was found on his clothing.

Clarke added that he later met Henderson and walked to Denton without meeting anyone who knew him. Clarke added that he knew Mr Eves had no money on him because of his inability to pay him his full wages and he would not therefore have entertained the thought of robbing his employer.

The jury listened carefully to all the evidence but were evidently not swayed by Clarke's story and returned a verdict of wilful murder against the two prisoners. The Coroner remanded both prisoners to the next Kent Assizes and the boys were taken back to the police station for the night. Here, much of their bravado had disappeared; Henderson was very dejected and, although Clarke initially put a brave face on it and tried to sing a song, he too finally broke down.

At the Kent Assizes in Maidstone the following January, Clarke and Henderson were tried for the crime alleged against them. The witnesses and evidence put forward by the prosecution were much the same as at the inquest and the remand hearing before the magistrates. Despite being a poor waterman whose simple home was a dilapidated rented building in Church Street, Henderson's father had managed to scrape enough money to pay for the services of a Mr Kingsford and Mr Biron, QC. Clarke, who had no money, was defended by Mr Dean, who was only asked by the judge to take on the case the day before the opening of the trial. Mr Dean apologized to the jury that his grasp of the evidence might not be all that he would have wished – not very encouraging for the poor wretch he was defending on a capital charge.

Mr Biron, for Henderson, was fortunately better prepared and, although he was unable to deny that his client had admitted that he and Clarke had carried out the assault with a stick, he sought to show that Henderson had been a mere onlooker – a contention supported by the lack of blood on his client's clothing. According to the learned counsel, Henderson had been invited to be present simply to witness the thrashing which Clarke intended giving his employer because of his perceived neglect of his wife.

The judge ably summed up the case at the end of the two-day trial, advising the jury that they had three choices open to them: they could find the prisoners guilty of murder, guilty of manslaughter or not guilty of either felony. In the end the jury returned a verdict of manslaughter, indicating that they did not believe the two lads intended to kill Thomas Eves, but merely meant to cause him some injury. This decision pleased the judge because it not only accorded with the evidence before the court but also relieved him of the dreaded task of passing the death sentence. Instead, the sentence on both prisoners was twenty years' penal servitude, and in Victorian England twenty years meant just that – no question of the sentence being halved for good behaviour; prison meant prison and hard labour meant exactly what it said, even in the case of two 16-year-olds.

Clarke and Henderson were sent to St Mary's Prison in Chatham, where the prisoners were mostly engaged in making bricks to be used in the extension of the nearby naval dockyard. The thought of spending the next twenty years in this rigidly disciplined place of punishment must have been a terrible prospect for such young lads but, as it happened, William Clarke only served four years as his health broke down and he died of tuberculosis at the age of twenty. Little is known of the fate of Charles Henderson; in 1893, when he was halfway through his sentence, the prison was closed and the convicts were dispersed to other gaols and all trace of Henderson has been lost.

The death of Thomas Eves, terrible though it was, was to prove merely the beginning of a whole catalogue of financial and personal disasters for the family. Mrs Eves moved out of Manor Farmhouse into a small terraced house in the Wrotham Road and died only two years after her husband. She was fifty years of age. The Subscription Grounds and Nurseries passed to Thomas Eves's sons by his first marriage, but they proved unequal to the task and the business closed within a very short space of time with most of the land being sold off for building. The Pavilion was dismantled and rebuilt in Milton Road, close to where it passes over the railway. No longer required as a theatre, the largely wooden building was taken into use by the Territorial Army and used as a drill hall until it was finally demolished in the 1970s to make way for the building of more houses.

Given the substantial income from the sale of the Pleasure Grounds for building, it might be expected that the Eves family would be set for a prosperous future, but the sons who proved incapable of managing their father's profitable business also failed to invest the proceeds wisely. The whole capital was very quickly frittered away and the violent death of Thomas Eves left nobody any better off: not his widow nor the rest of the Eves family, not the citizens of Gravesend, who lost a very popular and much valued asset, and certainly not Clarke, who spent the rest of his short life in prison, nor Henderson who spent most of his youth behind bars.

A grave end to a Gravesend story.

Chapter 17

Murder at the Sawmills

he Baltic Saw Mills Company was a thriving Tunbridge Wells business during the nineteenth century and had premises in Western Road, Goods Station Road, Commercial Road and Kensington Street. It was one of the most important employers of labour in the town in its heyday but, like so many other companies, it fell victim to the march of progress and went out of business in the twentieth century. Its imposing buildings were abandoned and eventually demolished to make way for other, new and more modern establishments.

But it was not its reputation as an employer or the wealth it brought to the town that was to be its memorial, but a vicious and wanton murder which occurred in 1888.

The Baltic Saw Mills, scene of the murder.

The company's engine man was a long-standing and loyal employee by the name of Bensley Cyrus Lawrence who lived in Mercer Street, where, on the night of 20 July that year, he was relaxing with his wife and thinking of retiring to bed. Suddenly there was an unexpected and unusual knock at the back door. Muttering the usual 'Now who can that be at this time of night?', Bensley Lawrence went to answer it. His wife heard a man's voice saying, 'Mr Potter wants you at *The Cypress*.' Mr Potter was the sawmill foreman and Lawrence's boss but was not the sort to ask his men to meet him in a public house. Mrs Lawrence knew this and remarked on the fact to her husband and the caller. The latter then changed his mind and said, 'No, you are wanted at the office.'

Fearing there had been a break-in or fire or some such calamity, Lawrence went to fetch his coat and left with the caller, down the enclosed passageway which led from his house to Goods Station Road. Mrs Lawrence never saw who it was at the door, nor did she recognize the voice. Time passed and Mrs Lawrence began to be concerned, so she sent her son, Bertie, to find his father and see what was keeping him. Bertie soon found his father outside the sawmills, talking to another man, whom he failed to recognize. On approaching the couple, Bertie was sent back home to fetch some matches as it was possible that Mr Potter, when he arrived, would want to go into the mill office and they would need to light a lamp. Bertie duly returned with the matches but still did not recognize the other man.

Around 10.40 that evening shots were heard and, shortly afterwards, Bensley Lawrence was carried back to the house from the sawmills, unconscious and bleeding from a head wound. He was taken to hospital where he died the next day from a bullet which had been fired at close range and had passed through the brain.

Lawrence was a well-known and well-respected man and the worthy citizens of the town were outraged. The Borough Police Force, under its long-serving chief officer, Superintendent John Joseph Embery, made diligent enquiries but to no avail. Lawrence appeared to have no enemies and there were no clues as to the perpetrator of this inexplicable murder. A reward of £100 was

Police Gazette *depiction of the incident.*

offered for information leading to the arrest of the killer but this too seemed to have no effect.

The investigation did discover two young boys, Frank Hemsley and Arthur Shoebridge, who were playing in the mill yard that evening. They told the police that they had seen two men come into the yard and, as they knew they were trespassing, they hid behind a stack of timber. The men were dressed in working jackets and fashionable bowler hats and the shorter of the two said, 'Now is your time. Be careful what you are at. I'll stop here.' Once the taller man had gone and the other had moved away, the two boys slipped out of the yard and made their way home, attaching no importance to the exchange they had overheard.

Other witnesses were found who said they had seen Lawrence talking to a man near the mill, the identity of whom was unknown. One of these witnesses heard Lawrence say to his companion, 'Where's Mr Potter? Where's he got to?' But Mr Potter had never sent the message and knew nothing of it. Was this companion the killer? If so, who was he? No one seemed to know and he was certainly not an employee of the mill or someone would have recognized him.

The case soon ceased to be of burning interest, as this was the time Jack the Ripper was prowling through the streets of London and his horrendous crimes eclipsed this little local murder. The first breakthrough in the Tunbridge Wells case came two months later, when a letter appeared in the *Tunbridge Wells Advertiser*:

Sir – Two months having now passed, I venture to ask you to be kind enough to allow me a small space in your valuable paper for a few facts concerning the death of the late Mr. Lawrence. In the first place I beg to state that all the evidence given at the inquest and afterwhers as been utterly false, with the exception of the two lads in the timber. I beg to correct the wrong statement that Mrs. Lawrence gave, for I, the murderer, did not summose [summons] *him from his house at all, as it was outside the backdoor when I first spoke to him, or my intension was to have shot him on the spot. Lawrence was very talkative when he was out of doors, little thinking of the death he had so shortly got to die. The last words he spoke when in my company was when he caught sight of the pistol sticking out of my pocket. He said, 'What do you carry them there sort of things about with you for?' My answer was, 'To shoot down dogs and curs like you.' (What, would you shoot a —.) Bang! and once more Tunbridge Wells was startled by another mistery which is never likely to be found out. I might here state that the key which was found on the spot is likely to lead to no clue whatever, as it is as much a mystery to me as the murder is to you. I also wish to threaten Mr. Edwards if he has any more to say conserning Mr. Martin, who is as inosent of the crime as he is.*

I remain, yours truly,
Another Whitechapel Murderer

Although the letter gave no clue as to the author, the depth of knowledge of the crime convinced the police that it was indeed written by the murderer and that he was still in the area.

A young boy, Walter Saunders, was found who said that a young man had given him a letter to take to the newspaper offices towards the end of September and that, although he did not know him, he would be able to identify him if he saw him again.

On 11 October 1888, a prayer meeting was held in the town's Salvation Army Citadel and an address was given by Captain Cotterill on 'Victories won; what they cost'. In response to the usual invitation, two lads, William Gower, an 18-year-old moulder at the sawmills, and Charles Dobell, a 17-year-old plumber, were the only two members of the congregation to go forward to the penitential table. Captain Cotterill noticed that Gower appeared to be having some difficulty as he prayed for around an hour 'without getting thoroughly saved'.

The following morning, the captain was surprised to receive a call at his house by Gower, who appeared to be troubled and anxious. In reply to the question, 'Did you get victory last night?', Gower replied, 'No, but my mate did. I have come to get saved this morning.' The captain was pleased that at least one of his penitents had been saved the previous night and that the other had now come to him to help him find God. But, although they prayed together for some time, Gower seemed unable to feel he had been saved. Captain Cotterill asked Gower if he had something on his mind and, after some hesitation, he said, 'There has been nothing bad done in Tunbridge Wells but what me and my mate were at the bottom of it. We've been two bad characters.'

Gower then went on to say, 'We were at the bottom of the Tunbridge Wells murder on July the twentieth.' This confession both took the captain by surprise and horrified him and, seeing the look on his face, Gower went on, 'Yes, me and my mate did it. We tossed up and the lot fell to him.'

The dumbfounded captain was used to confessions of all sorts of crimes and sins, from theft to blasphemy, from wife-beating to drunkenness, but this was a first. He said, 'Are you not sorry for what you have done?', to which Gower replied, 'Well, sometimes, but sometimes we feel that if he were to rise again, we should do the same thing.'

Not being bound by the confidentiality of the confessional, the horrified Captain Cotterill quickly contacted his superiors, who agreed that he could not possibly remain silent about what he had been told. Meanwhile, Gower penned a note to his friend Dobell:

My dear mate,

The Holy Ghost entered your heart last night. God only knows I wish it had mine. There seems to be something I could not give up. I went to the Captain this morning and confessed all to him. He wants to see us both tonight at six o'clock. I have not said anything to mother yet.

But having received the go-ahead from his superiors, Captain Cotterill wasted no time informing the police of what he had been told, and Superintendent Embery, who had been the head of the borough police for twenty-eight years after service in the Metropolitan Police, accompanied the captain to the sawmills. Gower seemed somewhat surprised at the sight of the policeman, but he shook hands with the captain and said, 'Well, I thought you would have waited till night.'

Potter, the sawmill foreman whose name had been used to lure Lawrence away from his fireside, was astonished when he was told the story. Dobell, whose finger it was on the trigger, was not employed at the sawmills. 'What grudge could he have had against

Stanley Road, Tunbridge Wells, where Gower lived at No. 34 and where the incriminating gun was found. The picture shows the houses with odd numbers, the other side of the street having been demolished and replaced by modern buildings.

Lawrence?' But Gower had a ready answer: 'He's a mate of mine and as true as steel.'

At the old police station in Calverley Road, Superintendent Embery questioned the prisoner closely: 'I have been told that you and Dobell either tossed or cast lots as to who should shoot Lawrence and that Dobell had to do it.'

'You're right,' said this rather cocky young man. 'It's quite true.'

Gower lived at 34 Stanley Road, very close to both Mercer Street and the sawmills, and the house was searched thoroughly. In an outhouse the police found a box containing a rather neglected revolver which had obviously been fired recently. All six chambers were loaded with rounds of live ammunition.

Dobell was arrested that evening and at first denied involvement in the killing but, on learning that Gower was already in custody and had confessed to the crime, Dobell agreed that he and Gower had cast lots to see who was to do the job, adding, 'You've got the murderer.' Both were charged with the wilful murder of Bensley Lawrence.

Under questioning, Gower admitted that he had a grudge against Lawrence, as he had reported him for lateness on no fewer than twenty-seven occasions, on each of which he was fined a penny by the management. Was this sufficient reason to take a man's life? Gower evidently thought so and his mate agreed with him.

While in prison on remand, the two Salvationists were visited by a large number of persons, both religious and philanthropic, including Salvation Army Major Mary Ann Ridsdale, no doubt hoping to save their souls. She offered them spiritual guidance and conversed with them and, on one occasion, she asked Gower what on earth had induced him to buy the revolver, to which he replied, 'I just wanted to be like other young men.' However, there is no evidence that the young bloods in Tunbridge Wells at that time were in the habit of secreting a firearm about their person, much less using it on anyone. It is much more likely that these not very bright young men were emulating their criminal heroes in the penny-dreadfuls which they bought and read avidly and discussed together at length. They would no doubt have been flattered to know that their story in pictures would soon feature in one of these.

While awaiting trial, both men readily admitted a string of further offences, including housebreaking, robbery and arson and, despite their young age, they were found to be persistent and hardened criminals. Despite this, Gower felt sure that, if he were to be reprieved, he could become a Salvation Army preacher.

The two men stood trial at the Kent Assizes in December 1888, indicted with being jointly involved in the murder of Bensley Lawrence. Their counsels put up a spirited and ingenious defence. Mr C H Richards, for Gower, blamed the Salvation Army for putting ideas into impressionable boys' heads and inducing them to confess to crimes which they had not committed. Mr C F Gill, for Dobell, claimed that there was no evidence that he had fired the fatal shot. It was true he had sent the letter to the newspaper (the boy he had given it to having already identified him) but this was simply an act of bravado with no foundation in truth. He too had been disturbed by the Salvation Army's uniforms, style of worship and ceremonials. But, with their confessions, there could be little doubt as to the outcome. Facing the assize judge and the bewigged and be-gowned counsels, there was a lack of the spirit of bravado which had so characterized their appearance before the magistrates at the remand hearing. Both, however, showed a passive indifference to their perilous position. In fact, they seemed to take a quiet delight in listening to the story of their guilt as it was unfolded before a rapt audience. Dobell was attired in a shabby tweed suit with his dark hair jauntily combed over his forehead, and the meaningless expression on his face did not give any clue as to his desperate character. Gower's boyish and clean-shaven appearance likewise gave no indication of the cunning villainy in which, on his own confession, he had been involved.

The trial was commendably brief and the jury retired for only twenty minutes before returning a clear verdict of guilty, but with a recommendation for mercy. The judge nevertheless donned the traditional black cap and sentenced the two wayward young men to death. There was to be no reprieve.

A new public executioner was now in post: the Yorkshireman and former policeman, James Berry, had taken on the job in 1884 and applied a new, more scientific approach to his grisly task. And so, on the first day of January 1889, Berry travelled down from Stafford, where he had just dispatched another murderer, to Maidstone Prison, where he was to attend to both Gower and Dobell the next day.

The enduring close friendship of these two lads was exemplified by a request made by Dobell to be pinioned ready for execution in the same cell as Gower. The executioner pointed out that this was not allowed but eventually it was agreed that he could tie Dobell in the cell corridor before bringing Gower out and doing the same to him, in the presence of his chum. They were then led off to the scaffold, where the deed was quickly accomplished and both young men departed this life together.

According to an article in *The Post*, Berry was of the opinion that neither lad should have been hanged:

Neither of the two boys could have been responsible for their crime inasmuch as they belonged to the degenerate type, and it would have been the more humane course to have sent them to Broadmoor, where there are several murderers who are much more sane than ever were the two lads.

The lads were romantically inclined, and wanted to be bandits, and according to those who investigated the crime privately the murder was the outcome of a boyish adventure. They certainly killed the victim of it, but whether or not they did so intentionally will never be known.

The £100 reward was offered to Captain Cotterill but he refused it, describing it as blood money, and suggested it should go to charity.

Chapter 18

The Child-Abducting Carrier

T he early days of the twentieth century saw Britain in something of a turmoil. After many years of comparative peace, the Army in South Africa was engaged in a war against the Afrikaans-speaking populace, who objected to the British plans for their country. It was not expected that this would be much of a problem to the great and glorious British Army, but this bunch of untrained, undisciplined and elusive farmers was conducting a very successful guerrilla war against the colonial power.

Added to this, the great Queen Victoria had just died, bequeathing the rule of the land to her somewhat profligate and pleasure-seeking son, Edward VII. Was this the beginning of the end of the great British Empire? Nowhere were these problems of state more keenly discussed than in Tunbridge Wells, that epitome of patriotic, royalist England (although not to become a 'Royal' Borough for another seven years) and nearby Tonbridge and Southborough.

But on the last day of the year 1901, a momentous event much nearer to home dumbfounded the people in the area. Around two o'clock that afternoon, 7-year-old Frances Eliza O'Rourke, the daughter of a tailor living at 15 Elm Road, Southborough, set out from home to deliver a package from her father to Mr Jenkinson's shop in Tunbridge Wells. The package duly delivered, little Frances set out on the return journey with another package around ten minutes past four but never arrived home.

As the hours slipped by, Mr O'Rourke became more and more concerned, and set off in search of her. He called at Mr Jenkinson's house and was told that the child had left soon after four o'clock, and so the distraught father notified the police, who carried out a search, hampered and curtailed, however, by the winter nightfall.

15 Elm Road, where the young victim lived.

Ye Olde Vauxhall Inn.

Ye Olde Vauxhall Inn *as it was around the time of the murder.*

Early the next morning, New Year's Day 1902, Thomas Dowse (or Doust) and Joseph Nye, woodcutters, were walking along Vauxhall Lane when they saw the body of a child in the Vauxhall Pond. Greatly alarmed, they hurried to the *Old Vauxhall Inn*, the only building in the vicinity, where they roused John Jeffries, the landlord, who accompanied them back to the pond. On arrival, John Jeffries waded in and pulled the lifeless figure out of the icy-cold water, but it was obvious that they were much too late to save her young life. The body was nearly naked, wearing only a vest and bodice, dark stockings and a pair of nearly-new lace-up boots. The clothing was tattered and torn. Mr Jeffries remarked that there was a clasp knife entangled in the girl's long hair and that there was a wound in the neck, below the ear.

The little body was carried to the stables at the inn, where it was later examined by Dr Watts. He concluded that the left jugular vein had been severed by two distinct stab wounds, causing almost instantaneous death, and that she had been sexually assaulted before death. Rigor mortis had only just begun to set in and the doctor concluded that death had occurred not many hours since.

Constable George Horton of the County Constabulary attended the scene and conducted an examination of the field and edge of the pond. He could find no footmarks in the soft earth but there were clear signs of wheel tracks outside the fence around the pond and also some hoof prints.

A further, more extensive search was called for, in the course of which Police Corporal Cassell found the girl's clothing in a heap in some bushes not far from the pond. There was also a man's handkerchief and a black mackintosh.

As it happened, only six years previously, the Kent County Constabulary had formed its first Detective Branch. Consisting of a sergeant and three constables, this was probably the first case of its kind and undoubtedly the most serious which the branch had so far had to deal with. The man in charge, Detective Sergeant Edwin Fowle (later detective inspector and ultimately a superintendent like his brother Thomas, and their father before them), arrived on the scene from his office in Maidstone with the rest of the detective force and reported to the local commander, Superintendent Styles. The full murder investigation was now set in motion.

An appeal for witnesses quickly brought fruit: Ethel Muggeridge, aged fifteen, said she knew Frances by sight and remembered seeing her on the road between Tonbridge and Tunbridge Wells, just down from the *Cross Keys Inn*, getting onto a four-wheeled horse-drawn van driven by a young man in dark clothing. Another young girl, Rose Dupond, gave a similar statement. Conrad Smith, a carman, said that around 4.45 pm on the evening in question, he had seen another carman, by the name of Harold Apted, driving along the London Road in the direction of Southborough. He did not speak to him but thought he saw a child on the van, but it was blowing and getting dark and he couldn't be sure. Other witnesses reported seeing a van, similar to that used by Apted, being driven at a furious pace from the direction of the Vauxhall Pond, towards Tonbridge.

Thomas Hawkins, a cabinet-maker, recognized the knife and said he had lent it to a young man by the name of Harold Apted some time before Christmas for the purpose of killing rabbits (and which Apted claimed to have lost some time ago). Another witness, Philip

The Cross Keys *public house in the 1950s.* Photo © copyright Kent Messenger Group.

Emery, a drover, said that he had seen Apted with a similar knife in Tonbridge Market on the day in question.

Who was this Harold Apted? It did not take the police long to identify him as a 22-year-old carman who lived with his parents at 69 Woodside Road, Tonbridge and who regularly drove his van between Tonbridge and Tunbridge Wells, acting as a general carrier. Detective Sergeant Fowle wasted no time in catching up with this young man and subjecting him to close questioning. Apted, of course, denied all knowledge of the murder. He claimed he never used the Vauxhall Lane route, but the evidence against him was piling up. There were bloodstains on Apted's coat, which he claimed he got in the slaughter house, and the van appeared to have been recently scrubbed out.

Detective Sergeant Fowle's mind was made up: this was his man and, at 6 pm on 3 January he arrested Apted and took him to Tonbridge Police Station, where he was formally charged with the murder of Frances O'Rourke.

A Home Office analyst, Dr Stevenson, said that the marks on Apted's coat were definitely blood, although he could not say whether they were animal or human. They were, however, definitely 'mammalian'. There was also blood on the straw and on pieces of wood removed from the floor of Apted's van, as well as blood and human hair on the knife (which, considering where it had been found, was hardly surprising).

At a hearing on 9 January 1902, the magistrates agreed that there was sufficient evidence to remand Apted for trial and so, at the end of February 1902, Harold Apted appeared before Mr Justice Wright at the Kent Assizes in Maidstone.

The prosecution's case was clear: on the day in question, the prisoner at the bar had driven his van to Tunbridge Wells, returning by a less-frequented route. Somewhere between Tunbridge Wells and Southborough he caught up with Frances O'Rourke and somehow induced her to get onto his van, possibly by drawing her attention to the fact that this would be a quicker and warmer way of travelling on such a cold, wintry day. Once on the van, Apted tried to rape the girl but, perhaps to stop her screaming and attracting the attention of passing workmen on their way home, stabbed her in the neck with the clasp knife he had earlier borrowed from Thomas Hawkins. He then tipped her body over the tailboard, into the pond. There was blood on the prisoner's clothing, although this had been smeared with grease, presumably in an attempt to disguise it, and the van appeared to have been thoroughly scrubbed out, but this had not completely removed traces of blood on the wooden floor and on the straw covering it.

Dr M J Watts was called and described the injury as a deep cut apparently made by a sharp knife of the type produced by the prosecution, being the one found in Frances's hair. A major blood vessel had been severed and death would have occurred very quickly.

Mr Hohler for the defence was quickly on his feet: 'Would you not have expected to find the clothes of the person who struck the blow on the deceased child covered with blood?'

'I should,' was the reply by the surgeon.

'Did you not tell Apted after you had examined him that he had no marks on his body, which would tell in his favour?' pursued the learned barrister.

'Yes,' was the response.

The doctor being the last witness for the prosecution, counsel for the defence rose to put his case and call his witnesses. The first witness was George Gilham of Tonbridge, who said he saw Apted return home to his stables at 4.40 pm. The next day he employed him to move some furniture and did not think the van had been washed out in the meantime.

Frederick Kisley, also from Tonbridge, said he saw Apted in Quarry Hill Road around 5.15 pm and again in the *British Volunteer* in Tonbridge at 5.30 pm.

Sidney Shepherd, an upholsterer employed by the first witness, Mr Gilham, said that when he returned to his work from his tea break between 5.30 and 5.40 pm, the van stood outside the stables. The next day he helped to load the van with furniture and he did not notice any blood.

Thomas Hinkley, the landlord of the *British Volunteer*, said he saw Apted in the bar around 5.15 pm and did not notice anything unusual about him. He only drank a soda.

Harold's father, Thomas Apted, testified that his son assisted him in his business as a coal and wood merchant. He arrived home for tea at 5.50 pm, left at 6.45 pm, and came back at 9.45 pm, when he went to bed.

Philip Adams was with the prisoner from 6.50 pm for about twenty-five minutes when he left him with a Miss Pool. Apted's behaviour was perfectly normal.

Mary Pool, an attractive young lady, said she was with Apted, whom she only knew slightly, from 7.15 pm until 7.45 pm.

Mr Hohler then addressed the jury. He pointed out that the prosecution had made a great point of fixing the time of the murder as being between 5 pm and 6 pm, even though Dr Watts, who saw the body the next morning, had opined that death had occurred some ten or twelve hours earlier, that is, between 9 and 10 pm. The purpose in bringing all the previous witnesses to give evidence was to prove that the prisoner's whereabouts between around 5 pm and 10 pm were known to a number of people and that he could not possibly have committed the murder within these times. Moreover, these defence witnesses were very clear in their evidence, unlike those put up by the prosecution.

The Crown's evidence, he claimed, was purely circumstantial and had failed to connect the prisoner with the murder. He found it extraordinary that the girl, Ethel Muggeridge, who said she saw Frances O'Rourke get onto the van, did not even know her name until after the murder. Neither she nor the other girl, Rose Dupond, could identify the van or its driver. There had been no suggestion as to how the murder had been committed and there was merely an assumption that the van seen in Vauxhall Road had anything to do with it. It was impossible for the girl to have been murdered on the van as it would have been 'deluged with blood' and, if she had been murdered on the ground, there would have been a large quantity of blood there. The police had been unable to find any such traces of blood as they might have expected. It was unreasonable to believe a murder had been committed on the high road at a time when workmen would be returning home. The prosecution had suggested that the body had been thrown from the van to the edge of the pond and one must question whether Apted was physically capable of such an action.

Mr Hohler said that Apted's conduct throughout had been that of an innocent man. It was extraordinary that there was no blood on the right side of his clothing, given that Dr Watts had surmised that the blow had been struck with the right hand and that blood would have spurted out and deluged the assailant. Of course there was blood on the floor of the van: it was occasionally used to convey calves' heads and it is very difficult to age bloodstains. Finally, would Apted have left the clasp knife in the girl's hair, knowing full well that it could easily be traced back to him?

Counsel for the Crown made its final address to the jury, emphasising that death had occurred between 5 and 6 pm, that Frances had been seen with a man in a van in Vauxhall Lane, and that if Apted was in Vauxhall Lane between 5.00 and 5.30 pm then he was the murderer.

It does seem, with the benefit of hindsight, that the Crown's case was an extremely thin one, and the assertion that if Apted was in

Vauxhall Lane at the relevant time he must be the killer was a somewhat extraordinary one. By modern standards it would be reasonable to assume that the case would be dismissed, but juries in the early Edwardian era were not so discriminating and the jury in this case returned a verdict of guilty within an hour, albeit with a recommendation for mercy in view of the prisoner's age. The death sentence was duly passed and it seems that the jury's recommendation for mercy was disregarded for, on Tuesday 18 March 1902, Harold Apted was hanged in Maidstone Prison for the murder of Frances O'Rourke. Such was the public interest in the case that a crowd of around 2,000 people gathered outside the prison, awaiting the signal that the death sentence had been carried out.

By now, hangings had been refined to the point where the slow and painful death by strangulation which so characterized executions in previous centuries was no longer the case, and Harold Apted died virtually instantaneously from dislocation of the vertebrae – that is, a broken neck.

But did he commit the murder for which his life was taken by the state? He does not appear ever to have made any form of confession, not even to the chaplain who attended him in the condemned cell. And on the very day that Apted was hanged, Alexander Moore, who lived in Prospect Road, Southborough, was charged with sending threatening letters to the parents of the murdered girl, threatening to kill them and their entire families. Was this the true killer and had there been a dreadful miscarriage of justice? We shall never know.

Chapter 19

Beware of Bathtime

or most of us, bathtime is regarded as a time for relaxation, a few moments of peace and quiet, a refuge from life's troubles and woes. But for an unfortunate few, bathtime was their last moment on this earth, and the key to this terrible situation was one George Joseph Smith.

Smith was born in Bethnal Green, London in 1872, the son of a respectable insurance agent. Unlike his parents, however, George Smith soon began to show criminal tendencies, and a string of comparatively minor offences led to his being sent to a reformatory in Gravesend at the age of nine.

He was released after seven years, presumably regarded as ready to lead an honest and God-fearing life, but this was not to be. Returning to live with his mother in Bethnal Green, Smith was soon in trouble again and received a number of short-term prison sentences for theft and receiving, culminating in a sentence of twelve months' hard labour for receiving property stolen by a female associate, whom he induced to steal for him.

Released from prison, he went to Leicester, where he opened a baker's shop and in January 1898 married 18-year-old maidservant Caroline Thornhill, much against her parents' wishes. Smith did not, however, marry her under his real name but used a pseudonym – a practice he was to employ many times in the future. The baker's business rapidly failed and Smith obtained various domestic service situations for his wife and encouraged her to steal for him. When she was finally caught trying to sell some spoons in Hastings, she was sentenced to prison for twelve months and, when she was released, she bitterly informed on her husband. As a result, in 1901 he too was imprisoned, in his case for two years.

In 1899, while his one and only legal wife was serving her prison sentence, Smith contracted another, bigamous, marriage to a highly respectable lady who ran a boarding house in London. When

Caroline left him and fled to Canada, he merely moved in with his other 'wife' before seizing all her savings and disappearing once more.

In June 1908 Smith married Florence Wilson, a widow from Worthing, after a whirlwind romance. Very shortly afterwards he inveigled £30 out of her and took her to an exhibition at the White City. He found her a seat and, telling her he was just going to get a newspaper, he walked out of her life for ever, pausing only to return to her lodgings in Camden and make off with all her belongings.

Using the proceeds from the sale of Florence's goods and chattels, some £80 or £90, Smith set himself up as a dealer in second-hand goods in Bristol, where he took on 28-year-old Edith Mabel Pegler as his housekeeper. Incredible as it may seem, in the same month as he had left Florence Wilson (July 1908), Smith employed, wooed and married Edith Pegler. In the course of the next few years' shenanigans, when Smith would absent himself from his latest bride for weeks at a time, 'on business', he would often return to Edith, who appears to have been his one true love, although he treated her far from well. What later proved to be of interest was the fact that, according to a statement Edith made to the police, Smith only once took a bath to her knowledge and showed little interest in the bathrooms in the various lodgings where they stayed.

In June 1909 Smith met Sarah Freeman in Southampton and went through a marriage ceremony with her in September of that year. Once 'married', he did the same to her as he did to Florence Wilson. After getting her to withdraw all her savings (£260) and sell some shares to finance his business as an 'antiques dealer', he took her out to the National Gallery for the day, made an excuse and disappeared, collecting her belongings from her flat, which he then sold. The £260 he had taken from Sarah Freeman he used to buy a property in Southend.

His next victim was 32-year-old Beatrice 'Bessie' Mundy. Up until now Smith's victims had all lost money and possessions but Bessie was to lose something even more valuable: her life. Smith used the alias of Henry Williams when he entered the life of this daughter of a deceased bank manager in Clifton, Bristol in 1910.

They were married in Weymouth in August of that year – yet another whirlwind romance and, yet again, the bride was a wealthy young woman, Bessie having been left £2,500 by her father. Although Bessie was unable to touch the money, which was held in a trust fund, she was entitled to the income from the invested money, which was paid in the form of an allowance of £8 a month. As she was not a big spender, there was an accumulated surplus of £138 due to her, which Smith lost no time in getting his hands on before performing his usual vanishing trick. This time he left his new wife a scurrilous letter, accusing her, quite untruthfully, of having given him a venereal disease.

Once again, Smith moved back in with Edith Pegler in Bristol but, by chance, bumped into Bessie again in Weston-Super-Mare in 1912. Going out one morning from the boarding house where she was staying, Bessie was astonished to see the man she believed to be her husband and whom she had not seen for eighteen months, on the sea front, 'looking over the sea'. No doubt this rather impressionable and romantically minded lady believed that this was fate and, such was the depth of her infatuation, she quickly forgave him and they were reunited.

After a period during which they moved around from place to place, the reconciled couple finally settled in Herne Bay, where Smith (or Williams as he was now calling himself) took a short-term tenancy of a house at 80 High Street, rented for the yearly sum of £18, payable monthly.

Smith, having discovered that he would not benefit from his wife's trust in the event of her death, consulted a solicitor about the possibility of revoking the trust. The latter felt the trustees, Bessie's uncle and her brother, would be unlikely to consent to a revocation under the circumstances and, if the wife died intestate, her estate would go to the next of kin under the Statute of Distributions, and the husband (who was not classed as the next of kin) would get nothing. The solicitor advised Smith to seek counsel's opinion as to what would be the situation were she to leave a will in his favour, and he to do likewise. Counsel's opinion was quite clear: the whole of her £2,500 capital would pass to her husband. And so Bessie's death warrant was signed.

Smith's next step was to acquire a second-hand bathtub, a simple affair without taps, haggling with the shopkeeper to get the price reduced by half a crown (12½p), though in the end he never paid for it.

Mrs Williams had been complaining of headaches, and so her husband took her to see a recently qualified, local general practitioner, Dr French, suggesting that his wife suffered from epilepsy. The doctor prescribed bromide of potassium. On Friday 12 July, Williams woke Dr French in the early hours, to say his wife was having another attack. The doctor attended and found nothing seriously wrong and called back the next afternoon, when Mrs Williams looked 'in perfect health'.

But around eight o'clock the following morning, Dr French received a note from Mr Williams which read, 'Can you come at once? I am afraid my wife is dead', and so he hurried to the house. There he found Bessie Williams still in the bath, her head submerged, with her legs stretched straight out before her, out of the water. There were no signs of violence and the Doctor deduced that Mrs Williams had drowned as a result of an epileptic fit, basing his opinion, no doubt, on the seeds of falsehood planted in his mind by Smith.

An inquest was held on the following Monday, presided over by Mr Rutley Mowll, the Dover solicitor, but the deceased's family, not having been notified of this, were not present and so were unable to express any misgivings or to seek an autopsy. The evidence was heard and the jury agreed with the doctor's diagnosis and returned a verdict of death by misadventure. The Coroner also awarded Mr Williams the sum of £2,579 as specified in the will Mrs Williams had made just five days before her death, which he spent on purchasing several properties in the Bristol area and buying an annuity for himself. Smith had finally managed to get his hands on the small fortune which had been so carefully held in trust for his late wife. Despite this windfall, Smith did not hesitate to return the bathtub to the shop to avoid having to pay for it.

Once again, Smith took up with Edith Pegler, inviting her to join him in Margate. He was now flush with money, despite quickly losing £600 in injudicious property deals, telling Edith he had made a good deal on some Chinese antiques. The two love birds stayed together for some time, but eventually Smith moved on to pursue his fictitious antiques business.

This time Smith went to Southsea where, with his habitual good fortune, he met up with a rather stout young woman of twenty-five who was acting as a nurse to an elderly gentleman there. Despite that fact that Smith appears to have demonstrated no strong religious beliefs, it seems the couple met at the chapel Alice Burnham attended. Within a few days Smith had proposed to Alice and been accepted.

The newly engaged couple went to visit Alice's parents near Tring but only stayed a few days, the visit being curtailed because the Burnham family found Smith so objectionable that the couple were asked to leave. Mr Burnham described Smith as a man of 'very evil appearance, so much so that he could not sleep while Smith was in the house, as he feared Smith was a bad man and that something serious would happen'. It is curious how Smith could so quickly beguile his young victims when it seems everyone else was repelled by him.

Alice Burnham and George Smith were married in Portsmouth and travelled to Blackpool for their honeymoon. By this time Smith had insured his bride's life for £500. He quickly got his hands on what little money she possessed and she made a will in his favour. In Blackpool they obtained lodgings with Mrs Crossley, ominously having rejected the first boarding house they called at on the grounds that there was no bath.

On the day following their arrival in Blackpool, 11 December 1913, Alice asked for a bath, which was prepared for her by Mrs Crossley and, soon afterwards, Smith told the landlady that he was unable to make his wife hear. They entered the bathroom to find Alice dead in the bath. A doctor certified death by drowning through heart failure when in the bath and the inquest jury returned a verdict of accidental death.

Smith left the town as soon as he could, pausing only to collect all the money due to him under Alice's will and the life insurance. Once again, with his pockets full of cash, Smith returned to Edith Pegler in Bristol. Although Alice's death was a carbon copy of that of Bessie Mundy, Smith had no fear of being found out. It was eighteen months later and hundreds of miles away from Herne Bay and he had used a different name. However, Mrs Crossley, the landlady, harboured a number of doubts about that affair and especially Smith's version of it.

After a brief period during which Smith and Edith Pegler moved around the south coast, Smith identified his next victim in the form of Alice Reavil, a domestic servant, whom he encountered in the late summer of 1914, soon after the outbreak of the Great War. Once again, there was a whirlwind courtship and, after only three or four days, Smith proposed and was accepted. The couple were married in Woolwich Register Office and, following his usual pattern, Smith (now going under the name of Charles James) quickly induced Alice to sell all her belongings, withdraw all her savings and pass them over to him to invest in an antique shop. Only five days after the marriage, Smith alias James took his bride to some gardens where he told her he was going to the lavatory. That was the last she saw of him until after his arrest. Alice lost everything except a few shillings and the clothes she stood up in, but at least she did not lose her life.

Smith once more returned to Edith Pegler in Bristol until, towards the end of that momentous year, 1914, he told her he was going to 'have a run around again before Christmas with another young fellow he had met in Clifton'. In fact, the 'young fellow' was Margaret Elizabeth Lofty, a 38-year-old spinster daughter of a clergyman, now deceased, whom he had met in Bath. Under the malign influence of Smith, Margaret Lofty took out a £700 insurance policy on her life and it is a measure of Smith's powers that this eminently respectable, God-fearing woman, no longer in the first flush of youth, told a number of untruths in order to obtain the insurance policy and to expedite its implementation. With the arrangements now complete, the couple were married in Bath on 17 December 1914, Smith giving the name of John Lloyd. After the ceremony the couple travelled to Highgate in London, where Smith had previously booked rooms, having carefully examined the bath, commenting, 'This is rather a small bath, but I dare say it is large enough for someone to lie in.'

Smith's conduct and appearance when booking the rooms so disturbed the landlady, a Miss Lokker, that she decided that, although he had left a deposit, she would not allow him to take the rooms when he next called the following Thursday. And so, when the newly-weds arrived around 3 pm, they were told that the rooms were not ready and that they should return at 6 pm. Smith became annoyed and turned nasty, but he nevertheless left their meagre luggage in the hall and departed.

As it happened, Miss Lokker and her partner, Mrs Heiss, having previously had problems with undesirable lodgers, had contacted Detective Sergeant Dennison about Smith and it was on his instructions that they told Smith to return at six o'clock, when the officer would be present to have a word with the couple. When 'Mr and Mrs Lloyd' arrived at six o'clock, Dennison was there and, without identifying himself, told them they could not have the rooms as they had not provided references. Smith, in a fury, said to his bride, 'They don't want us', and left to find alternative accommodation in Bismarck Road, Highgate, having first made sure there was a bath there.

The pattern now begins to repeat itself. Smith took his new wife to see a doctor on the evening of the wedding, intimating that there could be a history of fits, and then, the next day, they went to a solicitor's to make her will and she drew all her savings out of the Post Office savings bank.

At 7.30 pm that evening, 18 December 1914, Mrs Lloyd asked if she could have a hot bath and Miss Blatch, the landlady, later testified to hearing splashing coming from the bathroom, which was directly over the kitchen, and a sound which seemed like wet arms against the side of the bath. The noise ceased and Smith was heard to play 'Nearer My God To Thee' on the harmonium, after which he went out to buy some tomatoes. When he returned he called out to his wife and, getting no reply, went upstairs, calling out to Miss Blatch, 'My God, it's my wife! She doesn't answer. I do hope nothing has happened to her!' He then went into the bathroom, where he 'discov   Margaret dead in the bath.

The story now moves to New Scotland Yard, the headquarters of the London Metropolitan Police. In January 1915, Divisional

Detective Inspector Arthur Neil received a letter from Joseph Crossley, who ran the boarding house in Blackpool, enclosing two newspaper clippings. One related to the death of Margaret Lloyd, née Lofty, aged thirty-eight, who had been found dead in her bathtub at their lodgings in Highgate by her husband, John Lloyd. The other cutting, dated 1913, referred to the death in the Crossleys' boarding house in Blackpool of the woman named Alice Smith, née Burnham, who had been found dead in the bath by her husband George Smith. Mr Crossley found the similarity between the two deaths to be striking and worthy of further investigation.

Detective Inspector Neil went to the address in Highgate where Mrs Lloyd had met her unfortunate demise. The landlady said she had been surprised that Mr Lloyd had insisted on inspecting the bathroom first, before seeing the other accommodation. On measuring the bath, Neil found it to be between four and five feet in length (depending on the depth at which the measurement was taken) and he was surprised that Mrs Lloyd could have drowned in such a small bath, especially as it was only three-quarters full when she was found.

The Coroner confirmed that there were no marks of violence on the body, apart from a tiny bruise above the left elbow. However, it had been remarked that Mr Lloyd had shown little grief and had ordered the cheapest coffin available. Digging a little deeper, the detective discovered that Mrs Margaret Lloyd had made a will only three hours before she died, leaving everything to her husband. She had also withdrawn all her savings the same day. The plot thickened when the Coroner informed Neil that he had received an enquiry from the Yorkshire Insurance Company, who had insured Mrs Lloyd's life for £700, the beneficiary being her husband.

An enquiry made of the police in Blackpool revealed that the late Mrs Alice Smith had also taken out a life insurance policy, again naming her husband as the beneficiary, and he had carefully inspected the bathroom before taking the lodgings in that town.

Obtaining good descriptions of both 'Smith' and 'Lloyd', the detective inspector was convinced that they were one and the same person. He had the offices of Lloyd's solicitor watched and, when a man answering the description of Smith/Lloyd appeared, he was questioned. He admitted he was Lloyd but denied that he was Smith, and so Neil told him he was being arrested on suspicion of having committed bigamy. No doubt believing that the only charge facing him was the comparatively minor one of bigamy, Lloyd admitted that he was also George Smith.

At this point the services of the renowned Home Office pathologist, Bernard Spilsbury, were called upon. Margaret Lloyd's body was exhumed and Spilsbury confirmed that there was water in the lungs. He also confirmed that the only mark on the body was the small bruise on the left elbow. There were no signs of a heart attack or respiratory disease, but the death appeared to have been almost instantaneous, as if she had suffered a stroke. Not being completely satisfied, Spilsbury suggested that some experiments should be carried out and Neil arranged for the bathtub to be brought to the police station.

Despite all these investigations and examinations being carried out discreetly and almost secretly, the press got wind of them and articles began to appear, referring to the 'Brides in the Bath'. Such an article was seen by the officer in charge of the police at the seaside resort of Herne Bay, who was struck by the similarities of these two cases to the death which had occurred in that Kentish town.

The officer recalled that, at the beginning of 1912, a year before the death of Alice Smith née Burnham in Blackpool, a man going by the name of Henry Williams had rented a house at 80 High Street, for himself and his wife, Beatrice 'Bessie' Mundy, whom he had married in Weymouth in 1912. Some weeks later, he also took possession of the bathtub Smith had obtained on approval and in which Bessie Mundy had been found drowned.

Meanwhile, Bernard Spilsbury had gone to Blackpool to conduct a post mortem examination on Alice Smith née Burnham. The results were identical with those for Margaret Lloyd, and Spilsbury, somewhat baffled, had the bathtub sent to London pending further experiments.

The man in the photograph of Smith alias Lloyd which Detective Inspector Neil had sent to Herne Bay was identified as the man calling himself Henry Williams, and so Spilsbury also examined the

80 High Street, Herne Bay, where Bessie Mundy was drowned in the bath.

body of Bessie Williams. This time he did find sure signs of drowning: the presence of goose bumps on the skin. The bath in which she had died was also sent to London.

Bernard Spilsbury pondered hard and long over his findings. Bessie Williams was five feet seven inches tall and the bath only five feet long. If she had indeed suffered an epileptic fit, she would have stiffened and the pressure of her feet on the foot of the bath would have propelled her head and upper body out of the water by the sloping head of the bath. None of the subsequent symptoms of an epileptic fit would have resulted in her drowning – the bathtub was simply too small.

Suppose, however, that Henry Williams (alias Smith) had, in the guise of teasing and playfulness, taken hold of Bessie's ankles and pulled them up towards himself, simultaneously pressing down on her head, causing her upper body to slip down into the water? The sudden rush of water into her nose and mouth might cause shock and a sudden loss of consciousness. This would account for the lack of signs of force and the small amount of water in the lungs.

To test Spilsbury's theory, Detective Inspector Neil hired some experienced female divers of the same size and build as the victims. When he tried to push them under the water they struggled and, had he persisted, there would have been signs of violence on the body. And so he tried Spilsbury's theory, suddenly pulling on the feet of one of the divers. She immediately disappeared under the water, virtually without a struggle and Neil was concerned to note that she was no longer moving. She was quickly removed from the bath and resuscitated although it took Neil and a doctor more than half an hour to bring this experienced diver back to life. When she had recovered, she said the only thing she remembered was the sudden rush of water before she passed out. It seemed that Spilsbury's theory had been proved.

In all, between 1908 and 1914, Smith had entered into seven bigamous marriages under assumed names, in most cases stealing all the possessions of the 'wives' before vanishing. In between most of the marriages, Smith would return to Edith Pegler in Bristol or she would be invited to join him in some other town. The investigation by Detective Inspector Neil was meticulous and painstaking in the extreme, obtaining copies of all the wills, marriage certificates, bank records, and so on from the numerous places where Smith had conducted his nefarious affairs.

On 23 March 1915 George Joseph Smith was charged with the murders of Bessie Mundy, Alice Burnham and Margaret Lofty, and his trial at the Old Bailey began on 22 June, the indictments from Lancaster and Maidstone Assizes having been transferred to the Central Criminal Court under the so-called 'Palmer Act'. This law would only allow him to be tried for the murder of Bessie Mundy, although evidence relating to the other two murders was admitted by the judge to prove system (a propensity to commit a given crime using a certain technique), despite the objections of Smith's eminent counsel, Sir Edward Marshall-Hall. The judge advised the jury:

If you find an accident which benefits a person, and you find that the person has been sufficiently fortunate to have that accident happen to him a number of times, benefiting each time, you draw a very strong, frequently an irresistible, inference that the occurrence of so many accidents benefiting him is such a coincidence that it cannot have happened unless it is design. And it is for that purpose that the prosecution invite you to consider the circumstances of the deaths of Alice Burnham and Margaret Lofty.

In all, 264 exhibits were placed before the court during the trial and 112 witnesses, from forty different towns, were called to support the prosecution's case. There were no witnesses for the defence. It took the jury a mere twenty minutes to find Smith guilty of the murder of Bessie Mundy and he was duly sentenced to death.

A very robust appeal was lodged on his behalf by Smith's formidable defence team, based mainly on the lack of direct evidence incriminating Smith. The question of whether details of the deaths of Alice Burnham and Margaret Lofty should have been admitted by the judge as evidence of system was strongly contested but, in the end, the appeal was dismissed and George Joseph Smith was hanged at Maidstone Prison on 13 August 1915, by John Ellis, assisted by Thomas Pierrepoint.

Chapter 20

Mass Murder at Manston

Nearly a hundred years ago, during the First World War, an air station was brought into existence at Manston on the Isle of Thanet for the use of the Royal Naval Air Service. Just a small landing strip to start with, equipped with a handful of the flimsy scout (fighter) planes of the time, its importance grew over the years until, by the time of the Second World War, it was a major airfield which played a leading role in the Battle of Britain and, later, the Berlin Airlift.

Because of its situation so close to the continent of Europe, shot-up and otherwise disabled aircraft returning from operations over enemy territory made the airfield their first choice for emergency landings, despite its lack of a suitable hard runway. On one single night in 1942 there were fifty-six emergency landings, which included four complete Spitfire squadrons, four Wellington and four Stirling bombers. A new, long, surfaced emergency runway was called for and so, in that same year, at a cost of over £1,000,000, the destruction of a number of houses and the diversion of a main road, a new 3,000 yard hard runway, capable of handling the largest bombers and transport aircraft, was laid.

After the war, as well as continuing to be available for use as an emergency landing place, Manston was used by civil aircraft as well as the RAF and, in 1950, the Americans arrived in the form of the 20th Fighter Bomber Wing of the Strategic Air Command, which was to share the airfield with the RAF.

And this is where our story really begins.

Wednesday, 24 August 1955 was a bright, sunny day and, since this was before the days of cheap holidays abroad, Margate, Ramsgate, Broadstairs and the other seaside towns in Thanet were packed with summer tourists and visitors. The children were on holiday and sales of ice cream and candyfloss were booming. Just

The old control tower at Manston airfield.

ten years after the end of the Second World War, and with the Korean War apparently over, the population was more than ready to relax and laze in their deckchairs on the beaches from which they had been excluded during the war years.

From time to time the buzz of contented holidaymakers was augmented by the drone and whine of aircraft landing on and taking off from nearby Manston airfield, where, according to the *Daily Sketch*, there was 'a vast US air base'. And it was this presence which was soon to be responsible for a violent disruption of the peaceful scene.

Among the GIs stationed at Manston was one Napoleon Green, a 21-year-old black airman attached to the Airfield Police. He had something of a history of misbehaviour, but nothing remotely approaching that on which he was about to embark. He was facing a possible charge of theft and of assaulting a young girl, and it was perhaps this that was the trigger for his subsequent actions. It certainly appears that he had been in a peculiar frame of mind the previous evening, when he boasted to his room mates, 'Ah intend to mow down a few of you'se guys tomorrow, especially that bastard Ader.' Captain Ader was the Provost Marshal, the camp's senior 'policeman', before whom Green was due to appear for questioning. Green continued his ranting in the barrack room, saying, 'Now you listen to me, you'se guys. Tomorrow I shall die but I shall come to the mess hall at twelve o'clock and rub you all out.' His colleagues merely laughed, one or two tapping their temples, indicating that they thought Green was deluded; no one took his threats seriously.

On the morning in question, Green was due to work on the grounds with the airfield gardener, Leo 'Shorty' Thorn, but, before setting off from his hut, he scribbled a note on his locker saying 'Today, I die'. He met up with the gardener as instructed and began trimming the edges of the lawn surrounding the Officers' Mess but then suddenly darted off to an area of the camp to the west of the B2190 Manston to Margate Road. Here he made his way to the 'gun room' in the building which housed the Air Police

A group of US Air Police at Margate Police Station, where they had an office.

office and cells, where he was seen by Airman Third Class James Robert Hall, who was on duty there on his own. Hall subsequently told the inquest:

He went over to the stencil machine and started using it and banging about. I told him to quit before he broke it. He hit it four or five times. He seemed in a normal state of mind. I was busy counting sheets and blankets and then heard the click of a gun. It was the first time I saw him with a gun. He didn't say anything but walked over and picked up a holster. He walked towards the counter again and picked up a hatchet. I followed him towards the counter, then he went to the gun cage door and hit the lock with the hatchet. I told him to quit and said I'd get the key. Then I saw the note on the counter saying 'Today I die.' It was signed 'Napoleon Green'. I knew then there was something funny. All this time he had the pistol towards me and, after I said I was going to get the key, he pointed it right at me and said I was going to stay there. After he started banging, a different expression came on his face. He hit the lock of the cage again and took ammunition for the pistol and for a carbine, scooping up a handful and keeping the gun pointed at me. I turned my back and started talking to him. I heard him pick up the carbine. I turned round and he walked through the front door, taking the carbine and revolver, one in each hand. When he got out I reported to my sergeant who telephoned the Air Police. Five minutes later I heard shots being fired.

Outside the gun room, Green loaded the weapons, in the use of which he had been so well trained, and, stuffing his pockets with the spare rounds and magazines, made his way to the Air Force billet in Building 848.

Green kicked open the door to Hut 848, the pistol in his right trouser pocket and the carbine at the hip, shouting at the astonished off-duty airmen inside, 'Get out of here by ten o'clock or else, you bastards!' He then asked where Captain Ader was and was told he was in the laundry.

A fellow black airman, Airman Second Class Nelson Gresham, ran across to Green and pleaded with his 'brother' to drop the weapons before anyone got hurt. His reward was a single shot from the carbine discharged at point-blank range and the brave airman was dead before he hit the ground. Green then sprayed the room with automatic fire, wounding Airman Second Class Quannah Parker, fortunately not fatally, before rushing out of the billet, leaving the bewildered airmen staring after him. Green was by now running around in circles, shouting unintelligible threats and shooting at anyone who came too close to him, obviously utterly deranged.

Former RAF Warrant Officer Aubrey Easto was the camp's civilian tailor and was driving along Halley Road in his smart little Morris Minor, when he saw airmen rushing out of their billet, many still in their underwear. While he was musing what could be the cause of the commotion, there was a bang from the front of his car and he thought the engine had thrown a piston. In fact, the front offside tyre had been blown by a burst from Green's carbine. When he got out of the car to investigate, he was astonished to see the glass in the driver's door shatter as he closed it and, looking round, saw for the first time Green brandishing the carbine. Mr Easto quickly ran round the other side of the car and pulled his female assistant out of the front passenger seat. Together they crouched behind the car as Green ran off. Apart from a small graze to Easto's leg, they had both had a very lucky escape.

The next to suffer were two US airmen who were near one of the offices. Sergeant Gouvier was shot and slightly wounded while Airman Lester Hunt received a bullet to the chest which fortunately proved not to be fatal.

Green's next target was the Budget and Accounting office where, without provocation or warning, he opened fire at random, shooting Master Sergeant Lawrence Velasquez dead. Many of the pay office staff were local girls – typists, book-keepers, clerks, and so on – and one of these, Wendy Welton, watched horrified as the 34-year-old father of four fell to the floor. Screaming hysterically, she made a rush for the door but another bullet stopped her in her tracks, hitting her in the thigh.

Meanwhile secretary Margaret Shirley Hull was on her way from the office to the Commissary, when she saw a group of men running towards her along Halley Road, pursued by Green, who was discharging the carbine indiscriminately. On seeing her, he cried, 'Hey, I want you!' and, as she turned left down the Link Road, ran after her and caught her by the arm. 'Where are you going?' he demanded. She replied that she was on her way to work. He then asked her if she could drive a car but she said she couldn't. Green interrupted their conversation to fire a burst at some people sheltering in a doorway, loosening his grip on her arm. Margaret seized the opportunity to walk away towards the corner of the road but Green came after her and said, 'You're coming with me.'

'Who do you think you are, telling me where to go?' the brave girl replied, and attempted to get away again.

At this moment, Corporal Grayer of the RAF Police, who had been 'walking out' with Margaret Hull, came round the corner on his bicycle. Seeing her struggling with Green, he stopped and had just put his foot to the ground when Green deliberately turned the carbine on him and shot him in the left hip, the left side of the back and on the right side of the neck. It was later established that he died from shock and multiple haemorrhages and only lived a few minutes after the attack.

Despite being told by Green to leave the dying airman where he lay, Margaret went to comfort him, and Green left the scene, walking towards the airfield. On the way he came across Leo Thorn, with whom he had been working earlier, and said, 'Get out of the way, Shorty. I don't want to hurt you too.' 'Shorty' Thorn wasted no time complying with this instruction.

Green made his way towards the main gate, where he stopped an incoming van driven by Leonard Broadbent from Margate, ordering him and his four passengers to get out, but, before they could move, Green sprayed the side of the van with bullets from the carbine, riddling the vehicle from front to back. Miraculously, none of the occupants of the van was killed, although Ann Cockburn from Broadstairs was hit in the leg and Ian Yeomans from Ramsgate caught a bullet in the buttocks as he scrambled out of the van.

Presumably it had been Green's intention to make off in the van, but his wild and reckless shooting had made the vehicle undriveable, and so he carried on towards the main gate on foot, still waving his weapons and firing at anything which took his fancy. At the gate, Master Sergeant Rowley J McDaniels, USAF, was sitting in his new left-hand drive Ford Popular, unaware of the drama which had been unfolding within the camp. He was suddenly alerted by Green firing at an incoming car and then pointing the pistol at the sergeant's head, telling him, 'Ah'm not afraid of you, mister. You just do as you are told and drive like hell. You hear, man?' before climbing into the back seat. Wisely deciding that discretion is the better part of valour, the good sergeant did just that, and drove out of the gate towards Margate.

Sergeant McDaniels later told the inquest:

When we reached a crossroads just outside Margate, he said he wanted to go to London. I told him I was low on gas, which was true. By then I had started talking to this madman and I suggested that he might like to drive himself. This, I thought, would allow me to contact the police. To my surprise, he agreed and, after I had shown him the controls, I got out and ran like hell. I hitched a lift from a passing motorist and went straight to the police station. When I left the car, Green shouted out, 'Tell that bastard Captain Ader that when they get me boy, ah will be dead.'

In fact, as Green drove off alone down Nash Road, the police had already been alerted and a description of Green and the stolen car had been circulated and road blocks set up. Constable Tony Hunt, the Ramsgate Divisional motorcyclist, was alerted and made his way on the quiet but not very high-speed Velocette LE machine to the air base, where he was joined by Sergeant Charles Munson. Captain Ader outlined the situation and asked the two civilian police officers if they were armed. With a glance at each other, they solemnly drew their trusty wooden truncheons and replied, 'Yes, we are armed!'

Captain Ader was not particularly impressed and barked at one of his men, 'Get me a rifle! I'm going to get that guy!', and joined the posse which was being formed to give chase.

For some reason, Green parked the hijacked Ford car in Nash Road and continued on foot, still carrying the two weapons. Constable Bert Bridgland of the Kent County Constabulary was at his home in Nash Road near the crossroads, getting ready to go on duty, when his wife remarked that she had just seen a coloured

Constable Bert Bridgland (photo taken when he joined the Margate Borough Police before the Second World War).

American airman go past, carrying a gun. Bert told her not to be daft and continued lacing up his motorcycle boots but then saw Green walking back to where he had left the car. A few moments later the Ford Popular jerkily passed the police house 'as if it was being driven on kangaroo juice', heading towards Westwood. Shortly afterwards the constable answered the flashing light on the police pillar at 'Coffin Corner' at the top of Nash Road and, on being told what had occurred, mounted his motorcycle and went off in pursuit.

By now at least three jeeps full of armed US Air Force police were in pursuit, joined by the unarmed Constable Bridgland on his motorcycle. Green had now reached the town of Broadstairs, with its narrow streets packed with tourists and holidaymakers. Regardless of the imprecations hurled at him by narrowly avoided pedestrians, Green raced down Harbour Street and stopped outside the *Tartar Frigate* public house close to the harbour.

Ignoring the protests of 70-year-old Fred Beecham, the local car park attendant, who objected to Green leaving the car in the narrow street rather than in his car park, Green ran down the steps onto the beach. He did pause long enough, however, to call back to Fred, 'You tell them, old man, that if they want me, they'll have to come and get me.'

It was now 10.45 am and more than a dozen Kent police officers, some armed, were in pursuit, together with a large number of US military police. They had closed sufficiently on their quarry to be able to see him, stumbling over the rocks at the foot of the 20-metre-high cliffs, watched by an enthralled audience of

The Tartar Frigate *in Broadstairs.*

The beach at Broadstairs where Napoleon Green finally met his end at his own hands.

holidaymakers. Shots were fired both by Green and by his pursuers as they made their way for over a mile along the beach until, as Green neared the 'thirty-nine steps' leading up to a house once owned by a prominent Nazi, he stopped and walked into the sea. By the time the water reached his knees, Green knew the game was up. He was trapped, surrounded by civil and air force police so he slowly turned the carbine towards his chest and fired. One burst was enough and the fugitive dropped dead.

Constable Bert Bridgland was the first to reach the body, on which there were later found to be just three wounds: two near the heart and one on the right arm, the former having been made by a weapon fired at close range, that is, self-inflicted, while the third had been made after Green's death. Contrary to popular legend, the body was not 'riddled with bullets'.

And so Napoleon Green's threat or premonition had come true and he did indeed die that day, as did Airman Second Class Nelson Gresham, Master Sergeant Lawrence Velasquez and RAF Corporal Raymond Grayer.

Only by the greatest of good fortune did the death toll not exceed these three innocent parties, as it could so easily have done. As it was, seven more unfortunates were nursing their wounds, thankful they were not among the fatalities arising out of the 'Mass Murder at Manston'.

Index